Agni Purana

The Eternal Flame of Knowledge

Table of Contents

Introduction

• Overview of the Agni Purana

In the grand tapestry of Hindu philosophy and theology, the Agni Purana emerges as a blazing beacon, illuminating the path of knowledge, devotion, and cosmic order. Among the 18 Mahapuranas, this sacred text stands apart for its profound versatility, offering guidance that spans spiritual enlightenment, ritualistic practices, and practical knowledge essential for daily life. Rooted in the eternal flame of Agni, the god of fire, this Purana is both a repository of ancient wisdom and a testament to the transformative power of fire—the primordial force that sustains and renews the cosmos.

The narrative begins with a divine dialogue, a common yet powerful framework in Hindu scriptures. The Agni Purana unfolds as a conversation between Lord Agni and the sage Vasishtha, one of the seven great sages (Saptarishis). Agni, the eternal flame, serves not only as the deity of sacrificial fire but also as the embodiment of universal knowledge. His role as the cosmic mediator, bridging the mortal and divine realms, makes him an ideal narrator of this timeless scripture. Through this discourse, Lord Agni reveals profound truths, encapsulating the essence of dharma (righteousness), artha (material prosperity), kama (desire), and moksha (liberation)—the four purusharthas or aims of life.

The Agni Purana is vast in scope, comprising over 15,000 verses divided into 383 chapters. Its structure reflects the layered complexity of Hindu thought, seamlessly integrating mythology, theology, philosophy, and practical sciences. While its primary focus is spiritual guidance, the Purana is also a manual for worldly living, covering subjects such as architecture, astrology, medicine, and warfare. This blend of sacred and secular knowledge underscores the Hindu worldview, where the material and spiritual are not separate but interconnected, forming a harmonious whole.

Central to the Agni Purana is the concept of *dharma*, the universal law that governs all existence. Through its verses, the Purana elaborates on the duties of individuals across different stages of life (*ashramas*) and social orders (*varnas*). It emphasizes the importance of righteous conduct, self-discipline, and devotion as pathways to spiritual growth. By weaving dharma into every aspect of life, the Agni Purana reminds humanity of its intrinsic responsibility toward society, nature, and the divine.

The Purana also delves deeply into rituals and ceremonies, highlighting the significance of *yajnas* (sacrificial offerings) in maintaining cosmic harmony. In Hindu tradition, fire is not merely a physical element but a sacred medium through which offerings are conveyed to the gods. As the presiding deity of fire, Agni becomes the central figure in these rituals, symbolizing transformation, purification, and the unbroken connection between the earthly and divine realms.

Beyond spiritual teachings, the Agni Purana is a treasure trove of practical knowledge. It provides detailed instructions on temple construction, iconography, and the art of sculpture, reflecting the sophisticated architectural traditions of ancient India. It outlines principles of statecraft and governance, offering timeless advice for rulers on justice, diplomacy, and administration. The text also includes insights into astrology and astronomy, guiding individuals in understanding the celestial influences on human life. Additionally, it touches upon Ayurveda, the ancient science of life, presenting remedies and practices to ensure physical and mental well-being.

The Agni Purana's rich tapestry of narratives further enhances its appeal. Myths and legends woven into its verses serve not only as allegorical lessons but also as a source of inspiration. Stories of gods, demons, sages, and kings highlight the eternal struggle between good and evil, reinforcing the triumph of righteousness. These tales, brimming with symbolism, provide moral guidance while captivating the imagination.

What sets the Agni Purana apart is its accessibility and inclusiveness. Unlike some texts that cater exclusively to the priestly class, this Purana addresses a broad audience, encompassing householders, ascetics, and even rulers. Its teachings are universal, transcending social and cultural boundaries, making it a guide for all who seek knowledge and spiritual growth.

At its core, the Agni Purana is a celebration of fire—not just as a physical phenomenon but as a metaphysical principle. Fire represents energy, transformation, and illumination. It is the force that burns away ignorance, kindles the light of wisdom, and sustains the cycle of creation. In Hindu philosophy, fire is equated with the inner flame of consciousness, the divine spark that resides within every being. By invoking Agni, the Purana inspires individuals to nurture this inner flame, guiding them toward self-realization and union with the divine.

As we delve deeper into the Agni Purana, we are reminded of the timeless relevance of its teachings. In an age where humanity grapples with the challenges of materialism, environmental degradation, and spiritual disconnection, the wisdom of this ancient text serves as a clarion call. It urges us to rediscover our intrinsic harmony with the cosmos, to uphold dharma, and to kindle the eternal flame of knowledge within our hearts.

The Agni Purana is not merely a scripture; it is a living tradition, a spiritual companion that transcends the barriers of time and space. Its verses, like the ever-burning flame of Agni, continue to illuminate the path of seekers, offering solace, guidance, and inspiration. As we embark on this journey through its sacred teachings, we are invited to partake in the eternal dance of fire—a dance that unites the mortal and the divine, the earthly and the eternal.

• Importance in Hindu scriptures

Among the vast ocean of Hindu sacred texts, the *Agni Purana* holds a unique place, its significance woven deeply into the fabric of spiritual, philosophical, and cultural traditions. It is not merely a scripture; it is a guide, a torchbearer illuminating countless aspects of human existence. From its profound theological insights to its practical wisdom on worldly matters, the *Agni Purana* encapsulates the essence of Hindu thought, making it an indispensable pillar of the vast corpus of Indian spirituality. Its importance lies not only in its teachings but also in its ability to bridge the material and spiritual worlds, uniting them into one harmonious continuum.

The Purana as a Source of Eternal Knowledge

Hinduism, being one of the oldest religions in the world, does not rely on a single text or prophet. Its vast library of knowledge spans the *Vedas*, *Upanishads*, *Sutras*, *Epics*, and *Puranas*. Among these, the *Puranas* serve as a critical link between the esoteric, complex philosophies of the Vedas and the more accessible, narrative-driven teachings for the common devotee. The *Agni Purana*, in particular, stands out for its remarkable breadth, addressing both sacred and secular knowledge with equal reverence.

As its name suggests, the *Agni Purana* is narrated by Lord Agni, the god of fire and the intermediary between the divine and mortal realms. Fire, as a symbol of purification, energy, and transformation, embodies the very essence of the Purana's teachings. By revealing the eternal truths to Sage Vasishtha, Agni transforms abstract, cosmic principles into practical wisdom that can be applied to everyday life. This makes the *Agni Purana* an invaluable scripture for seekers of all kinds—those pursuing spiritual liberation as well as those striving for worldly success.

The Role of Agni in Hindu Thought

To fully grasp the significance of the *Agni Purana*, one must first understand the centrality of Agni in Hindu philosophy. Agni, the eternal flame, is one of the most revered deities in the Vedic pantheon. In the *Rigveda*, Agni is described as the mouth of the gods, the carrier of sacrificial offerings, and the witness to all human actions. He is not just the physical fire but a cosmic force—present in the hearths of households, in the fires of yajnas (sacrificial rituals), and in the spiritual fire that burns within every soul.

The *Agni Purana*, therefore, is not just a text; it is an embodiment of this divine flame. It acts as a conduit through which humanity connects to the divine, channeling the transformative energy of Agni into the realms of knowledge, devotion, and action. Its teachings are not confined to specific rituals or doctrines but extend to the universal principles that govern life itself.

A Comprehensive Guide to Dharma

One of the *Agni Purana's* most significant contributions to Hindu scriptures is its detailed exploration of *dharma*, or righteous living. Dharma, in Hindu philosophy, is the cosmic law that sustains the universe, governing the moral and ethical duties of individuals, societies, and the cosmos. The *Agni Purana* serves as a manual for understanding and upholding this law. It provides guidance on the duties of various social classes (*varnas*) and life stages (*ashramas*), ensuring that every individual can align their actions with the universal order.

Through vivid stories, allegories, and prescriptions, the *Agni Purana* illustrates the consequences of adhering to or deviating from dharma. These teachings not only reinforce the importance of ethical conduct but also emphasize the interconnectedness of all beings. In doing so, the Purana transcends individual concerns, presenting a vision of life that is holistic and universal.

The Intersection of the Sacred and the Secular

Unlike many other scriptures that focus primarily on spiritual matters, the *Agni Purana* offers a remarkable blend of the sacred and the secular. It delves into subjects as diverse as temple architecture, iconography, statecraft, astrology, and medicine. This inclusivity reflects the Hindu worldview, where the material and spiritual dimensions of life are seen as complementary rather than opposing forces.

For example, the *Agni Purana* provides detailed instructions on the construction of temples and idols, emphasizing their role as conduits for divine energy. It also discusses the principles of governance, outlining the qualities of an ideal ruler, the administration of justice, and strategies for maintaining social harmony. By addressing such practical concerns, the Purana ensures that its teachings are relevant not only to ascetics and scholars but also to householders, kings, and commoners.

Spiritual Liberation through Fire Worship

At its heart, the *Agni Purana* is a spiritual text, guiding individuals toward liberation (*moksha*). It places special emphasis on fire worship, particularly through *yajnas*, as a means of attaining this goal. Fire is seen as a purifier, burning away the impurities of the mind and soul, and as a mediator, carrying prayers and offerings to the gods. By participating in these rituals, devotees not only honor the divine but also cultivate inner discipline and devotion.

The *Agni Purana* also highlights the symbolic significance of fire in meditation and self-realization. Just as fire transforms wood into ash, spiritual practices fueled by the inner flame of consciousness transform ignorance into wisdom. This metaphor resonates deeply in Hindu thought, inspiring seekers to nurture their inner light and strive for union with the divine.

A Text for All Ages

The timeless relevance of the *Agni Purana* is perhaps its most remarkable feature. Its teachings are not bound by the cultural or historical context of its composition but address universal truths that remain applicable across ages. In times of moral confusion and spiritual disconnection, the Purana serves as a beacon of hope, reminding humanity of its intrinsic connection to the divine.

Its narratives, filled with symbolism and moral lessons, continue to inspire devotion and introspection. Its practical wisdom, ranging from health and governance to art and architecture, remains a valuable resource for modern society. By bridging the past and the present, the sacred and the secular, the *Agni Purana* exemplifies the enduring vitality of Hindu scriptures.

Conclusion: The Eternal Flame of Knowledge

The *Agni Purana* is much more than a scripture; it is a living tradition, a sacred fire that continues to burn brightly in the hearts of devotees. Its significance in Hinduism lies not only in its teachings but also in its ability to transform lives, illuminating the path of knowledge, devotion, and righteous action. As a source of spiritual and practical wisdom, the *Agni Purana* remains an eternal flame, guiding humanity toward the realization of its highest potential.

• Themes of knowledge, dharma, and cosmic order

In the vast ocean of Hindu sacred literature, the *Agni Purana* emerges as a blazing lighthouse, its eternal flame illuminating profound themes of knowledge, dharma, and cosmic order. These interconnected ideas serve as the backbone of the text, shaping its narratives and teachings while reflecting the essence of Hindu philosophy. The *Agni Purana* weaves these themes into a timeless tapestry, uniting spiritual and worldly wisdom, inspiring seekers to harmonize their lives with the eternal rhythm of the cosmos.

Knowledge: The Eternal Flame of Wisdom

Knowledge (*jnana*) is the bedrock of the *Agni Purana*. From its very beginning, the Purana establishes itself as a source of both sacred and secular wisdom, embodying the Hindu ideal of *sarva vidya maya jagat*—the universe as a manifestation of knowledge. Narrated by Agni, the deity of fire, the text itself symbolizes the transformative power of knowledge. Just as fire burns away ignorance and purifies, the teachings of the *Agni Purana* ignite the mind, illuminating the seeker's path toward truth and self-realization.

The Purana's approach to knowledge is holistic, encompassing not only spiritual truths but also practical sciences. It expounds on the mysteries of the cosmos, unraveling the secrets of creation, sustenance, and dissolution. Through vivid allegories and profound metaphysical discussions, it reveals the nature of *Brahman*, the ultimate reality, and the interconnectedness of all existence. This cosmic perspective invites readers to look beyond their limited selves, urging them to seek the eternal knowledge that transcends the transient world.

Equally significant is the Purana's practical wisdom. It offers guidance on architecture, astrology, medicine, and governance, presenting knowledge as a tool to improve worldly life. For instance, the chapters on temple construction and iconography emphasize not only technical precision but also the spiritual significance of sacred spaces. The text's discussions on statecraft reflect a deep understanding of human nature, offering timeless principles for justice and diplomacy. By integrating sacred and secular knowledge, the *Agni Purana* underscores the Hindu belief that all learning ultimately serves the greater purpose of aligning oneself with the cosmic order.

Dharma: The Pillar of Righteous Living

Dharma, the universal law that sustains the cosmos, is one of the central themes of the *Agni Purana*. Rooted in the Sanskrit root "dhr" (to uphold or sustain), dharma encompasses moral, ethical, and social duties. In the *Agni Purana*, dharma is not presented as a rigid set of rules but as a dynamic principle that adapts to individual roles, circumstances, and stages of life.

The text meticulously outlines the *dharma* of various social classes (*varnas*) and life stages (*ashramas*), offering a framework for righteous living. It emphasizes that dharma is not limited to religious rituals but extends to every aspect of life, from personal conduct to societal responsibilities. A king's dharma, for example, involves protecting his subjects and upholding justice, while a householder's dharma focuses on supporting their family and contributing to society. By addressing the duties of rulers, priests, warriors, and commoners alike, the *Agni Purana* ensures that no aspect of life is devoid of moral guidance.

Through its vivid stories, the *Agni Purana* illustrates the consequences of adhering to or deviating from dharma. Tales of virtuous kings, devoted sages, and selfless sacrifices serve as moral exemplars, inspiring readers to uphold righteousness in their own lives. Conversely, stories of those who stray from dharma reveal the inevitable suffering and chaos that arise when cosmic order is disrupted. These narratives are not mere moral lessons; they are reflections of the eternal truth that dharma is the foundation of harmony—within the individual, society, and the cosmos.

The *Agni Purana* also explores the spiritual dimension of dharma, presenting it as a pathway to liberation (*moksha*). By living in accordance with dharma, individuals align themselves with the divine will, purifying their minds and cultivating detachment from worldly desires. This spiritual discipline leads to self-realization, enabling them to transcend the cycle of birth and death. In this way, the *Agni Purana* elevates dharma from a mere ethical code to a profound spiritual principle, guiding individuals toward the ultimate goal of human existence.

Cosmic Order: The Rhythm of the Universe

Underlying the themes of knowledge and dharma is the grand vision of *rita*, the cosmic order that governs all existence. In Hindu cosmology, *rita* is the principle that maintains harmony in the universe, ensuring the regular cycles of nature, the balance of forces, and the interdependence of all beings. The *Agni Purana* celebrates this cosmic order, portraying it as a divine symphony orchestrated by the gods and sustained through human actions.

Agni, as the narrator of the Purana, embodies the energy that sustains *rita*. Fire, the element he represents, is both a physical force and a spiritual symbol of transformation and balance. Through the rituals of *yajna* (sacrifice), humans participate in the cosmic order, offering their gratitude to the gods and receiving their blessings in return. The Purana emphasizes that these rituals are not mere formalities but sacred acts that uphold the harmony of the cosmos.

The text also delves into the cycles of creation, preservation, and destruction, revealing the dynamic nature of *rita*. It describes how the universe emerges from the cosmic waters through the creative power of Brahma, is sustained by the preserving energy of Vishnu, and eventually dissolves into the fiery embrace of Shiva. These cycles are not random but governed by the divine intelligence of *rita*, ensuring that destruction is always followed by renewal.

Human actions play a vital role in maintaining or disrupting this cosmic order. The *Agni Purana* warns that when individuals or societies deviate from dharma, they create imbalance, leading to suffering and chaos. Conversely, acts of virtue, compassion, and selflessness reinforce the cosmic harmony, benefiting not only the individual but the entire creation. By emphasizing this interconnectedness, the Purana inspires readers to see themselves as integral parts of the cosmic web, responsible for its well-being.

The Interconnection of Themes

The brilliance of the *Agni Purana* lies in its seamless integration of knowledge, dharma, and cosmic order. These themes are not isolated but deeply interconnected, each enriching and supporting the others. Knowledge illuminates the path of dharma, guiding individuals to make righteous choices. Dharma, in turn, sustains the cosmic order, ensuring harmony and balance. And the cosmic order provides the framework within which knowledge and dharma operate, reflecting the unity of the universe.

Through its teachings, the *Agni Purana* invites readers to align their lives with these eternal principles. It portrays existence as a divine dance, where every thought, word, and action contributes to the cosmic rhythm. By nurturing the flame of knowledge, upholding dharma, and honoring the cosmic order, individuals can transcend their limitations and realize their oneness with the infinite.

Conclusion: The Eternal Wisdom of the *Agni Purana*

The themes of knowledge, dharma, and cosmic order are the lifeblood of the *Agni Purana*, infusing its teachings with timeless relevance and universal appeal. In a world often marked by ignorance, discord, and imbalance, these principles offer a path of hope, harmony, and enlightenment. The Purana reminds us that we are not mere spectators of the cosmic drama but active participants, entrusted with the sacred duty of preserving its beauty and balance.

As we delve into the sacred flame of the *Agni Purana*, we are invited to rediscover these eternal truths, to kindle the light of knowledge within, and to walk the path of dharma with courage and conviction. In doing so, we become co-creators of the cosmic order, aligning ourselves with the infinite rhythm of the universe and embracing our divine destiny.

Section 1: Origins and Structure

1. The Source of the Flame

- Mythological origins of the Agni Purana

In the ancient, hallowed corridors of Hindu mythology, where deities converse with sages and the cosmos reveals its secrets to the deserving, lies the origin of the *Agni Purana*. It is a tale as ancient as time itself, a narrative woven with the threads of cosmic mysteries, divine will, and the unyielding pursuit of knowledge. The *Agni Purana*, much like the element it is named after—Agni, the fire god—emerges from the interplay of the heavens and the earth, blazing with wisdom and illuminating the spiritual landscape for seekers across generations.

The story of the *Agni Purana's* creation is deeply intertwined with the primordial forces of the universe and the role of Agni, the celestial flame, as a divine mediator. Fire, in Hindu cosmology, is not merely a physical phenomenon but a sacred bridge between the mortal and the divine. It consumes offerings, carries prayers to the heavens, and returns blessings from the gods. Agni, as the embodiment of this elemental power, becomes the narrator of the *Agni Purana*, the keeper of its profound wisdom, and the conduit through which humanity receives its teachings.

Agni: The Divine Messenger and Narrator

The mythological origin of the *Agni Purana* begins with Agni himself, one of the most revered deities in the Vedic pantheon. Agni is the very essence of life, the divine spark present in all creation. In the ancient hymns of the *Rigveda*, he is invoked as the first priest, the one who sustains the cosmic order (*rita*) through the sacred fire ritual (*yajna*). His presence in the Vedic texts is both pervasive and intimate, a constant reminder of the divine energy that animates the universe.

It is said that Agni, in his eternal journey through the cosmos, gathered the knowledge of the gods, sages, and the elements. He listened to the secrets whispered by the winds, absorbed the wisdom of the earth, and witnessed the celestial dance of the stars. His flame burned with the light of a million truths, each one waiting to be revealed to humanity. Yet, for ages, this knowledge remained hidden, guarded by Agni's blazing form, until the moment of its revelation arrived.

The *Agni Purana* finds its origins in a cosmic dialogue, a divine exchange of wisdom between Agni and the great sage Vashistha. This meeting, according to legend, occurred in a time when the earth was shrouded in spiritual ignorance, and humanity yearned for guidance. Vashistha, a seer of unparalleled wisdom and one of the seven *Saptarishis*, approached Agni in his luminous form, seeking the knowledge that could restore balance and righteousness to the world.

The Meeting of Agni and Vashistha

The encounter between Agni and Vashistha is described as a moment of cosmic significance. In the quiet sanctity of a forest hermitage, where the air hummed with the energy of the divine, Vashistha sat in deep meditation. His mind reached out to Agni, invoking the deity through sacred chants and offerings. The fire before him roared to life, its flames leaping skyward as Agni appeared in his resplendent form.

Agni, the celestial flame, recognized the sage's intent and spoke with a voice that resonated like thunder yet carried the warmth of a comforting hearth. "O Vashistha," he said, "you, who are the keeper of the eternal truths, have called upon me. What is it that you seek?"

Vashistha, with folded hands and a heart brimming with reverence, replied, "O Agni, guardian of the cosmic flame, humanity stands at a crossroads. Ignorance clouds their minds, and dharma wavers under the weight of chaos. I seek the wisdom that can guide them back to the path of righteousness, that can rekindle the flame of knowledge within their hearts."

Moved by the sage's selfless plea, Agni agreed to reveal the sacred knowledge he had long guarded. " shall bestow upon you the teachings that encompass the cosmos," he declared. "These truths, preserved in the eternal flame, shall become the *Agni Purana*. It shall be a beacon of light for those who seek knowledge, dharma, and liberation."

The Cosmic Revelation

What followed was a revelation of cosmic proportions. Agni began to narrate the *Agni Purana*, his words weaving a tapestry of divine wisdom. He spoke of creation, describing how the universe emerged from the primordial waters through the will of the Supreme Being. He recounted the tales of gods and demons, their battles reflecting the eternal struggle between good and evil. He detailed the principles of dharma, offering guidance on righteous living for kings, priests, and commoners alike.

Agni's teachings were not confined to spiritual matters. He delved into the sciences, sharing knowledge of astronomy, medicine, and architecture. He explained the construction of temples, the symbolism of deities, and the significance of rituals. Every word was a spark of enlightenment, igniting the mind and soul of the sage who listened.

As the narration progressed, Vashistha realized that the *Agni Purana* was not merely a collection of teachings but a reflection of the cosmic order itself. Its chapters mirrored the cycles of creation, preservation, and dissolution, its stories carried profound allegories, and its instructions bridged the material and the spiritual.

The Sacred Flame Passed to Humanity

Once the narration was complete, Vashistha vowed to preserve and propagate the *Agni Purana* for the benefit of all beings. He transcribed the teachings, passing them on to his disciples and future generations. Through his efforts, the *Agni Purana* became an enduring legacy, a scripture that transcended time and space.

The mythological origins of the *Agni Purana* underscore its divine authority and timeless relevance. By attributing its knowledge to Agni, the eternal flame, the text emphasizes the transformative power of wisdom. Just as fire consumes and purifies, the teachings of the *Agni Purana* burn away ignorance, illuminating the path to truth and harmony.

Conclusion: The Eternal Flame of Knowledge

The story of the *Agni Purana's* origin is more than a myth—it is a profound metaphor for the journey of knowledge from the divine to the human realm. It reminds us that wisdom is not a human creation but a gift from the cosmos, entrusted to us through the medium of sacred texts and enlightened sages.

As we delve into the *Agni Purana*, we become part of this ancient legacy, kindling the flame of knowledge within ourselves and carrying it forward for future generations. Through its mythological origins, the *Agni Purana* invites us to reconnect with the eternal truths that sustain the universe, reminding us that we, too, are sparks of the divine flame.

- Connection with Lord Agni

Amid the vast pantheon of Hindu deities, each symbolizing distinct aspects of existence, Lord Agni stands out as the primal force of transformation, the link between the mortal and the divine, and the eternal messenger carrying the prayers of humanity to the heavens. The *Agni Purana*, named after this resplendent deity, embodies his essence—blazing with the light of knowledge, searing away ignorance, and nurturing creation through its sacred teachings. The connection between the *Agni Purana* and Lord Agni is not merely titular; it is a profound relationship that underscores the text's spiritual and cosmic significance.

Agni: The Embodiment of Cosmic Energy

In the Vedas, Agni is more than a deity; he is a cosmic principle. He is the life force pulsating in every atom, the spark that ignites existence, and the fire that sustains the universe. From the hearths of ancient homes to the grand sacrificial altars of the Vedic priests, Agni's presence was both intimate and universal. He was invoked as the intermediary, the one who accepted offerings and delivered them to the gods, ensuring the continuity of the cosmic cycle.

The *Agni Purana*, attributed to this divine flame, reflects Agni's multifaceted role in the universe. It is a scripture that illuminates not just the outer world of rituals and dharma but also the inner landscape of the soul. The text, much like its namesake, burns with truths that purify, enlighten, and transform. But to truly grasp the connection between the *Agni Purana* and Lord Agni, one must delve into the myths, metaphors, and cosmic roles associated with this deity.

The Divine Role of Agni as a Mediator

The mythological connection between Lord Agni and the *Agni Purana* is rooted in his unique position as the eternal mediator between humans and the gods. According to Vedic tradition, Agni is the first recipient of all sacrifices. When an offering is placed in the fire, it is Agni who consumes it, transforming it into smoke and energy that ascends to the heavens. This act of mediation symbolizes the transfer of material desires and prayers into the realm of the divine.

In the same way, the *Agni Purana* serves as a bridge between the mortal realm and higher wisdom. Through its verses, it delivers divine knowledge to humanity, illuminating the path of dharma and offering a guide to transcendence. Just as Agni carries sacrificial offerings to the gods, the *Agni Purana* carries the teachings of the cosmos to seekers of truth.

The Purana itself acknowledges this role of Agni in its narratives. It speaks of him not only as the narrator of the text but also as its essence, the eternal flame that lights the way for humanity. The teachings contained within the *Agni Purana* are presented as emanations of Agni's divine wisdom, making the scripture an extension of the deity himself.

Agni as the Narrator: A Symbol of Knowledge

The choice of Agni as the narrator of the *Agni Purana* is deeply symbolic. In Hindu thought, fire represents clarity, illumination, and transformation—all essential aspects of knowledge. Agni, as the fire god, embodies these qualities in their purest form. His flame pierces through darkness, revealing hidden truths, and his heat refines and purifies, burning away impurities and ignorance.

The act of Agni narrating the Purana to sages signifies the transmission of knowledge from the divine to the human. This is not a passive process but an active, dynamic exchange, much like the flickering of a flame that interacts with its surroundings. Agni's role as the narrator highlights his identity as the ultimate teacher, one who does not merely share information but transforms the seeker through the process of learning.

According to tradition, Agni revealed the teachings of the Purana to the sage Vashistha as a means of restoring balance in the world. At a time when dharma—the cosmic order—was threatened by chaos and ignorance, these teachings emerged as a beacon of hope. By attributing the text to Agni, the Purana emphasizes its divine origin and its purpose as a tool for rekindling the spiritual flame within humanity.

The Symbolism of Agni in the Purana

Agni's connection to the *Agni Purana* is further underscored through the text's themes and symbolism. Fire, in Hinduism, is not just a physical element but a representation of spiritual aspiration and transformation. The flame of Agni symbolizes the soul's journey—rising upward, striving toward liberation, and illuminating the path for others.

The *Agni Purana* reflects this symbolism in its teachings. It covers a vast array of topics, from cosmology and rituals to ethics and governance, each one aimed at kindling the inner flame of understanding. The text mirrors Agni's nature as both a destructive and creative force. Just as fire burns away the old to make way for the new, the *Agni Purana* challenges existing notions and invites readers to embrace higher truths.

For instance, the Purana's sections on dharma emphasize the importance of righteous living as a means of maintaining the cosmic order, much like how a controlled fire sustains life without causing harm. Its teachings on rituals highlight the transformative power of devotion, akin to the way fire transforms offerings into divine blessings. Even its discussions on architecture, medicine, and governance reflect Agni's role as a nurturer of life, providing the knowledge needed to create a harmonious society.

Agni as the Eternal Witness

Another profound connection between Lord Agni and the *Agni Purana* lies in Agni's role as the eternal witness. In Hindu rituals, fire is invoked as the witness to vows, symbolizing the unwavering presence of the divine. Whether it is a wedding, a yajna, or a coronation, Agni's flame stands as a testament to truth and sincerity.

Similarly, the *Agni Purana* serves as a witness to the eternal truths of the universe. Its verses capture the essence of cosmic laws, offering guidance that transcends time and space. By attributing the text to Agni, the Purana underscores its authority as a keeper of these eternal truths.

The Purifying Fire of Knowledge

Perhaps the most profound connection between Agni and the *Agni Purana* is their shared purpose as purifiers. Just as fire cleanses and purifies, the teachings of the *Agni Purana* aim to purify the mind, heart, and soul. The text challenges ignorance, dispels illusions, and invites readers to embrace a life of wisdom and virtue.

This purifying aspect is evident in the Purana's emphasis on self-discipline, ethical conduct, and devotion. It teaches that true knowledge is not just about acquiring information but about transforming oneself into a vessel of truth. In this sense, the *Agni Purana* mirrors Agni's role in the cosmos, serving as a force of spiritual transformation.

Conclusion: The Flame That Illuminates Eternity

The connection between the *Agni Purana* and Lord Agni is a testament to the transformative power of divine wisdom. Through this sacred text. Agni continues to fulfill his cosmic role, guiding humanity toward light, truth, and liberation. Just as his flame burns eternally, so too does the knowledge of the *Agni Purana*, illuminating the path for seekers across the ages.

In every verse of the *Agni Purana*, one can feel the warmth of Agni's presence, the spark of his wisdom, and the power of his transformative flame. It is not merely a scripture but a living embodiment of the divine fire, a beacon for those who seek to ignite the eternal flame of knowledge within their own hearts.

2. Composition and Content

- Chapters and major themes

The *Agni Purana*, a timeless scripture radiating with divine light, is a treasury of knowledge spanning myriad subjects. Like a vast ocean, its depths reveal the pearls of ancient wisdom, while its waves carry the essence of cosmic truths to the shores of human understanding. Comprising over 15,000 verses, this Purana is a remarkable confluence of myth, philosophy, science, and devotion. To dive into its chapters is to embark on a journey through time and space, uncovering profound insights that shape not just spiritual understanding but also practical living.

Let us walk through the structure and themes of the *Agni Purana*, unraveling its multi-dimensional essence, chapter by chapter, theme by theme.

An Ocean of Wisdom Divided into Streams

The *Agni Purana* is composed in the form of a dialogue between Sage Vashistha and Lord Agni. This conversational style makes the text both engaging and profound, allowing the wisdom of the divine to flow seamlessly into the realm of human thought. While its chapters span numerous disciplines, the underlying unity is unmistakable: the pursuit of charma, cosmic harmony, and ultimate liberation.

The Beginning: Invocation and the Eternal Flame

The text begins with an invocation, a sacred homage to Lord Agni as the eternal flame of creation, destruction, and sustenance. This sets the tone for the rest of the Purana, which unfolds as a tribute to Agni's divine role as the bearer of wisdom and the mediator between the terrestrial and celestial realms. Agni imparts the teachings to Sage Vashistha, not as rigid dogma, but as living truths adaptable to the ever-changing tapestry of life.

Themes Interwoven Through the Chapters

1. Cosmology: The Mysteries of Creation

One of the earliest sections of the *Agni Purana* delves into cosmology, describing the origins of the universe. It portrays creation as a divine act, orchestrated by Lord Brahma, where Agni plays a crucial role as the spark of life. The text speaks of the five elements—earth, water, fire, air, and ether—each contributing to the intricate dance of creation. Fire, as the primal energy, is exalted as the force that animates the cosmos.

Through metaphors and allegories, the Purana explains the cyclical nature of time, the yugas (epochs), and the cosmic dissolution (*pralaya*). These teachings are not merely academic; they inspire the reader to see life as part of a greater cosmic order.

2. Dharma: The Foundation of Existence

Dharma is a recurring theme throughout the *Agni Purana*. It is presented not as a rigid set of rules but as the living principle that governs the universe. Chapters devoted to dharma explore its various facets, from personal ethics to social responsibilities. The Purana provides guidelines for kings, householders, ascetics, and even warriors, emphasizing that dharma is the cornerstone of harmony in all spheres of life.

Particularly notable are the sections on *Rajadharma* (the duties of kings) and *Grhasthashrama Dharma* (the duties of householders). These chapters weave a vision of a balanced society where individuals uphold righteousness in their roles, contributing to the collective good.

3. Rituals and Worship: The Sacred Pathway

True to its association with Lord Agni, the *Agni Purana* places great emphasis on rituals, sacrifices (*yajnas*), and the proper methods of worship. It explains the significance of fire rituals as a means of connecting with the divine, purifying the self, and fulfilling desires.

Agni's dual role as the devourer of offerings and the deliverer of blessings is illustrated in meticulous descriptions of various yajnas, including the *Agnihotra* and *Ashvamedha*. Each ritual is infused with spiritual symbolism, reminding practitioners that offerings are not just material but an act of surrender and devotion.

The Purana also elaborates on the worship of different deities, including Vishnu, Shiva, and Devi, each representing distinct aspects of divinity. These chapters guide the seeker in establishing a personal connection with the divine, tailored to their inclinations and needs.

4. Philosophy: The Path to Liberation

In its philosophical sections, the *Agni Purana* transcends the realm of rituals to explore the ultimate goal of life—liberation (*moksha*). It discusses the nature of the soul (*atman*), the illusion of the material world (*maya*), and the means to overcome bondage. The teachings align with the *Vedanta* school of thought, presenting a monistic view where the individual soul is ultimately one with the Supreme.

Through vivid analogies and profound insights, the Purana guides seekers toward self-realization. It emphasizes that while rituals and dharma are essential for worldly harmony, true freedom lies in transcending dualities and realizing the oneness of existence.

5. Knowledge and Sciences: Illuminating Practical Life

One of the most fascinating aspects of the *Agni Purana* is its extensive coverage of practical knowledge. Unlike many spiritual texts that focus solely on metaphysical themes, this Purana delves into subjects such as:

- **Astronomy and Astrology:** Detailed descriptions of celestial bodies, their movements, and their influence on human destiny.

- **Architecture (*Vastu Shastra*):** Guidelines for building homes, temples, and cities in harmony with natural forces.

- **Medicine (*Ayurveda*):** Insights into maintaining physical and mental health, including herbal remedies and preventive care.

- **Martial Arts (*Dhanurveda*):** Training in the use of weapons and strategies for warfare, underscoring the balance between strength and wisdom.

These chapters reflect the holistic vision of the Purana, where spirituality and practical knowledge are intertwined, each enhancing the other.

6. Mythology and Stories: A Treasury of Inspiration

Interspersed with its teachings are captivating stories and myths that illustrate the principles of dharma, devotion, and divine grace. From the heroic deeds of avatars like Rama and Krishna to the sagas of sages like Vishwamitra and Valmiki, the Purana brings its lessons to life through narrative. These stories are not mere entertainment; they serve as allegories, inspiring readers to embody the virtues they depict.

One notable tale is the story of King Harishchandra, whose unwavering commitment to truth and dharma is a shining example for all. Another is the legend of the churning of the ocean (*Samudra Manthan*), symbolizing the eternal struggle between good and evil and the rewards of perseverance.

7. Esoteric Knowledge: The Mystical Dimension

The *Agni Purana* also delves into esoteric subjects, including mantras, yantras, and the secrets of tantra. These chapters explore the power of sound, symbols, and sacred geometry in unlocking spiritual potential. The Purana emphasizes that such knowledge must be approached with reverence and discipline, as it holds the power to transform both the individual and the universe.

The Unifying Flame: Themes of Harmony and Order

Throughout its chapters, the *Agni Purana* weaves a unifying vision of life as an intricate tapestry where every thread—be it spiritual, moral, or material—has its place. It upholds the cosmic order (*rita*), encouraging humanity to live in harmony with the divine, nature, and each other. Its teachings are timeless, relevant across eras, and adaptable to the complexities of modern life.

Conclusion: A Scripture for All Seekers

The *Agni Purana* is not merely a religious text; it is a guide to existence itself. Its chapters and themes resonate with the eternal quest for meaning, blending the spiritual with the practical, the mythical with the philosophical. As one reads its verses, the flame of Agni burns brightly within, illuminating the path to wisdom, harmony, and liberation. It is a text for kings and sages, householders and ascetics—a testament to the universal relevance of its divine teachings.

- Relationship with other Puranas

In the vast cosmos of Hindu literature, the *Agni Purana* stands as one of the many celestial gems that illuminate the infinite sky of spiritual wisdom. Yet, like stars that belong to the same constellation, the *Agni Purana* is intricately linked to its fellow Puranas, forming a harmonious network of interwoven knowledge. To truly understand its significance, one must delve into its relationship with the other 17 *Mahapuranas* and the broader Purana tradition, where each text complements the other, creating a unified tapestry of divine wisdom.

The Purana Tradition: An Interconnected Cosmos

The word *Purana* itself signifies "ancient" or "timeless," embodying the idea of eternal truths that transcend eras. The Puranas were designed to be accessible to all, including those unable to engage with the intricate *Vedas*, making them invaluable repositories of mythological, spiritual, and practical wisdom. While each Purana has its distinct focus and flavor, their unity lies in their shared goals: to teach dharma (righteousness), *artha* (material well-being), *kama* (desires), and *moksha* (liberation).

The *Agni Purana*, while primarily associated with Agni—the divine flame and mediator of cosmic offerings—is not an isolated narrative. It draws upon and contributes to the larger Purana tradition, reflecting shared themes, mutual references, and overlapping stories. This interconnectedness enriches not just the *Agni Purana*, but the entire corpus of Hindu mythology, philosophy, and devotion.

A Dialogue with the Other Puranas

1. Shared Mythologies: The Eternal Threads of Stories

The Puranas often recount the same mythological events, but each offers unique perspectives. The *Agni Purana* frequently aligns with and expands upon the narratives found in texts like the *Vishnu Purana*, *Bhagavata Purana*, and *Shiva Purana*. For instance:

- **Creation Myths:** The *Agni Purana* recounts the origin of the universe in alignment with the cosmogonic narratives of the *Brahmanda Purana* and *Vishnu Purana*. However, it emphasizes the role of Agni as the primal energy that sustains creation, adding a fiery lens to the shared cosmic vision.

- **Churning of the Ocean (*Samudra Manthan*):** This iconic story appears across multiple Puranas, including the *Agni Purana*, *Bhagavata Purana*, and *Padma Purana*. The *Agni Purana* highlights Agni's indirect role in preserving balance during the churning, portraying him as the subtle force that fuels divine actions.
- **Legends of Vishnu and Shiva:** The *Agni Purana* delves into the avatars of Vishnu and the cosmic dance of Shiva, echoing themes from the *Bhagavata Purana* and *Shiva Purana*. Yet, it often connects these deities to Agni, showcasing the interconnectedness of divine forces.

In this way, the *Agni Purana* acts as both a standalone text and a complementary piece of a larger puzzle, offering new dimensions to shared stories while reinforcing the unity of the Purana tradition.

2. Philosophical Synergy: Exploring Dharma and Moksha

The *Agni Purana* aligns philosophically with texts like the *Vishnu Purana*, *Bhagavata Purana*, and *Garuda Purana*. These Puranas collectively address the four goals of life, but each brings its unique perspective:

- **Dharma:** While the *Agni Purana* emphasizes practical aspects of dharma—rituals, kingship, and social duties—it resonates with the *Vishnu Purana*'s portrayal of dharma as the foundation of cosmic order. Together, they create a holistic understanding of righteous living.
- **Moksha:** Liberation is a recurring theme across Puranas. The *Agni Purana* shares the Vedantic vision of moksha with the *Bhagavata Purana*, emphasizing devotion, self-knowledge, and surrender to the divine as the ultimate path to freedom.

Through such philosophical dialogues, the *Agni Purana* complements and amplifies the teachings of its counterparts, creating a unified framework for spiritual seekers.

3. Rituals and Practices: A Shared Repository

The Puranas are renowned for their detailed guidance on rituals, festivals, and worship. The *Agni Purana*, true to its fiery essence, focuses on fire rituals and sacrifices, but it also references and elaborates on practices mentioned in other Puranas:

- **Fire Worship:** The *Agni Purana* provides an exhaustive account of *yajnas* (sacrificial rituals), aligning with similar descriptions in the *Brahmanda Purana* and *Markandeya Purana*. However, it uniquely emphasizes Agni's central role as the mediator of offerings, bridging the mortal and divine realms.
- **Temple Worship and Iconography:** Like the *Padma Purana* and *Vishnu Purana*, the *Agni Purana* discusses the construction of temples and the consecration of idols. Yet, it incorporates Vedic principles of geometry and energy flow, highlighting Agni's role in sanctifying sacred spaces.

- **Mantras and Tantra:** The esoteric teachings of the *Agni Purana* resonate with the tantric traditions found in texts like the *Devi Bhagavata Purana*. Its emphasis on the power of sound and symbols reflects the shared mystical undercurrent of the Puranic tradition.

4. A Universal Narrative: Complementing and Contrasting

While the *Agni Purana* often aligns with other Puranas, it also offers distinct perspectives that enrich the collective narrative:

- **Focus on Agni:** Unlike most Puranas, which primarily revolve around Vishnu, Shiva, or Devi, the *Agni Purana* places Agni at the center. This unique focus highlights the foundational role of fire in rituals, creation, and spiritual transformation, offering a complementary lens to the broader tradition.

- **Practical Knowledge:** The *Agni Purana* stands out for its encyclopedic nature, covering subjects like Ayurveda, Vastu Shastra, and Dhanurveda in detail. While other Puranas touch on these topics, the *Agni Purana* provides a more comprehensive guide, making it a practical resource alongside its spiritual teachings.

A Tapestry of Harmony

The relationship between the *Agni Purana* and other Puranas is not one of competition but of complementarity. Together, they form a vast tapestry of knowledge where each thread, though distinct, contributes to the whole. The *Agni Purana* shines as the flame that illuminates this tapestry, connecting its strands and revealing their collective brilliance.

In this web of interconnection, the *Agni Purana* reminds us of the unity underlying diversity—not just within the Puranas but within life itself. It teaches that all paths of knowledge, when pursued with sincerity and devotion, ultimately lead to the same divine truth.

Section 2: Agni's Role in the Universe
3. Agni: The Divine Mediator

- Agni as the bridge between gods and humans

In the boundless expanse of creation, where the realms of mortals and gods exist as parallel dimensions, there lies a sacred flame—a bridge that connects the earthly and the divine, the transient and the eternal. This flame is Agni, the primordial fire, revered not just as an elemental force but as a divine being who holds the universe together in a delicate dance of exchange and harmony. Agni is not merely a deity of fire; he is the cosmic messenger, the eternal mediator, and the invoker of sacred communion between gods and humans.

The Flame Born of the Cosmos

The story of Agni's role as a divine mediator begins in the primordial moment of creation. In Hindu cosmology, Agni was born from the cosmic churning, emerging as the first spark of life, light, and energy. In the dark void of pre-existence, it was Agni who ignited the process of manifestation. Fire, in its essence, became the vital principle of the universe—transforming the unmanifest into the manifest, the invisible into the tangible.

Agni's sacred task was clear from the beginning: to serve as the conduit between realms. His flames carried the offerings of the earthly to the divine and brought back the blessings of the gods to humanity. This dual role was not merely functional; it was symbolic of the eternal reciprocity that binds all of existence.

The Sacred Ritual: A Path to the Divine

In the ancient Vedic tradition, the ritual of *yajna* (sacrifice) became the central act of human devotion, and Agni its indispensable agent. Imagine a tranquil Vedic altar, adorned with sacred offerings—clarified butter (*ghee*), grains, and fragrant woods. As the priest chants mantras in rhythmic precision, the offerings are placed into the sacrificial fire. The flames rise, crackling and glowing, as the smoke spirals upward, carrying the prayers and devotion of humanity into the celestial realm.

This act is not merely symbolic but a profound expression of cosmic law. Through Agni, the offerings are transformed into an ethereal form, accessible to the gods. He becomes the sacred courier, ensuring that humanity's devotion reaches its intended divine recipient, whether it is Indra, the god of rain, or Saraswati, the goddess of wisdom.

The texts describe Agni as the *havya-vahana*—the carrier of offerings. Without him, the link between mortals and the divine would collapse, severing the flow of blessings, wisdom, and protection that sustains human life. Thus, every sacrificial flame is more than fire—it is Agni himself, present in his divine form, fulfilling his cosmic duty.

Agni: The Voice of Humanity

As the bridge between realms, Agni is often described as the "mouth of the gods" (*deva mukha*). In this role, he does more than carry offerings; he translates human intentions and prayers into the language of the divine. The mantras chanted during rituals are sacred vibrations, but it is Agni who ensures their potency and delivery. He deciphers the sincerity of the devotee, refining the raw emotions and desires of humanity into pure, divine energy.

This role positions Agni as not just a carrier but as a mediator who interprets and refines. Just as fire purifies gold, Agni purifies human devotion, stripping it of impurities and presenting it in its most pristine form to the gods. He becomes the ultimate arbiter, ensuring that the exchange between humans and the divine remains sacred and unbroken.

The Return Flow: Blessings and Prosperity

Agni's mediation is not a one-way process. Just as he carries offerings to the heavens, he also brings divine blessings back to the earthly realm. These blessings manifest as rain for crops, wisdom for guidance, and protection from adversities. In the Vedic worldview, this cyclical exchange is the essence of *rita*, the cosmic order. Without Agni, this sacred reciprocity would falter, plunging the world into chaos.

In times of drought or calamity, the absence of Agni's mediation is felt deeply. Ancient texts describe kings and sages performing intense fire rituals to reestablish this divine connection, invoking Agni to rekindle the flow of blessings. His flames, once reignited, symbolized the restoration of harmony and balance.

Agni as a Universal Mediator

Agni's role extends beyond Vedic rituals and mythology. In the *Mahabharata*, during the iconic *Khandava-daha* episode, Agni devours the Khandava forest to restore his strength, a narrative that underscores his relationship with humanity and the divine. Here, Agni is not just a receiver of offerings but a being with needs and desires, reflecting the human-like reciprocity between mortals and gods.

Even in the *Ramayana*, Agni plays the role of a divine witness and mediator during Sita's trial by fire. In this context, his flames become the ultimate arbiter of truth, bridging the human concept of justice with the divine ideal of purity.

The Symbolism of Agni: The Bridge Beyond Rituals

Agni's mediation is not confined to external rituals; it also has profound internal significance. Within the human body, Agni is represented by the digestive fire, or *jatharagni*, which transforms food into energy. Similarly, the inner fire of consciousness, *kundalini*, symbolizes spiritual awakening and the connection between the earthly and the divine within oneself. These internal manifestations of Agni mirror his cosmic role, reminding humanity that the bridge to the divine exists within as well as without.

Agni in the Modern World

Even in today's world, Agni's role as a divine mediator remains relevant. Fire continues to be a central element in Hindu ceremonies—be it the lighting of a *diya* (lamp) during Diwali, the sacred flames of a wedding, or the funeral pyre that guides a soul to the next realm. Each flame carries the essence of Agni's ancient role, bridging worlds and ensuring the continuity of life, death, and rebirth.

The Eternal Flame of Connection

Agni, the divine mediator, is not just a figure of mythology; he is the living flame that binds humanity to the gods. He is the messenger, the purifier, and the sustainer of the sacred exchange that defines existence. Through him, the mortal reaches the immortal, the finite touches the infinite, and the earthly merges with the divine. In every flicker of fire, in every ritual flame, Agni whispers the timeless truth: that humanity and divinity are forever connected, bound by the sacred bridge of the eternal flame.

- Significance in Vedic rituals

The world of the Vedas—the most ancient and revered scriptures of Indian civilization—is a realm of profound wisdom, intricate philosophy, and sublime rituals. The Vedic rituals, deeply embedded n the spiritual and cultural fabric of the Indian subcontinent, are more than mere ceremonies. They are the means through which humanity seeks to connect with the cosmos, align with natural laws, and transcend the mundane to achieve higher states of existence. To truly understand their significance is to embark on a journey that traverses the mystical andscapes of history, philosophy, and spirituality.

The Foundation: A Quest for Cosmic Harmony

The Vedic rituals, or **Yajñas**, are born from a fundamental principle that resonates throughout the Vedas—the concept of **Ṛta** (cosmic order). The ancient sages, or **ṛṣis**, perceived the universe as an intricately woven tapestry of interconnected energies. Every element of creation, from the celestial bodies to the smallest grain of sand, was believed to be governed by Ṛta, an eternal rhythm of balance and harmony. Human beings, as part of this cosmic order, were seen as participants in the grand symphony of existence.

The Vedic rituals were designed as acts of reciprocity—offering back to nature and the divine what humanity had received. This idea is eloquently encapsulated in the concept of **Yajña**, which translates to "sacrifice" but carries a deeper meaning of selfless offering. The rituals were seen as a bridge connecting the human and the divine, the microcosm and the macrocosm.

The Sacred Stage: An Environment of Purity and Precision

A Vedic ritual is a grand orchestration of meticulous details, reflecting the profound respect the ancient sages had for the divine. The stage for these rituals is not merely a physical space but a sacred environment meticulously prepared to resonate with spiritual energy.

Every element, from the construction of the altar (**vedi**) to the selection of offerings (**havis**), is governed by precise guidelines. The altar itself, often constructed in geometric shapes like a square or a lotus, is symbolic of cosmic principles. It is oriented in alignment with cardinal directions, signifying harmony with the natural world.

Purity is paramount in these rituals—not just of the space but of the participants as well. The priests, or **hotṛ**, are required to undergo rigorous purification processes involving fasting, meditation, and rituals to cleanse their minds and bodies. The participants, too, prepare themselves mentally and physically, recognizing that the ritual is a sacred act that demands their undivided attention and reverence.

The Instruments of Divinity: Mantras and Fire

At the heart of every Vedic ritual lies the **Agni**, or sacred fire. Agni is not just a physical flame but a divine messenger, a conduit between the mortal and the immortal realms. The fire consumes the offerings and carries their essence to the deities, establishing a direct link between the human and the divine.

The offerings, which may include clarified butter (**ghee**), grains, herbs, and even symbolic sacrifices, are carefully chosen to represent gratitude and devotion. They are placed into the fire with specific **mantras**, the sacred hymns of the Vedas. These mantras are not mere words but potent vibrations imbued with spiritual power. Each mantra is a sonic expression of divine truth, meticulously crafted to invoke specific deities and cosmic forces. The rhythmic chanting of mantras creates a sacred soundscape, believed to harmonize the vibrations of the environment with the higher energies of the cosmos.

Types of Vedic Rituals: A Spectrum of Sacred Acts

The Vedic rituals span a vast spectrum, from daily offerings to elaborate ceremonies lasting several days or even weeks. Each ritual serves a distinct purpose, addressing the diverse needs of human existence.

1. **Nitya Karma (Daily Rituals):** These are simple, obligatory rites performed daily by individuals to maintain spiritual discipline and connect with the divine. Examples include the **Agnihotra**, a small fire ritual conducted at sunrise and sunset.

2. **Naimittika Karma (Occasional Rituals):** These rituals are performed on specific occasions, such as eclipses, solstices, or significant life events like marriage or childbirth. For instance, the **Vivaha Yajña** is the Vedic marriage ceremony, a sacred union not just of two individuals but of their spiritual destinies.

3. **Kāmya Karma (Desire-Fulfilling Rituals):** These are optional rituals performed to fulfill specific desires, such as prosperity, health, or victory in battle. The **Putrakameshti Yajña**, for instance, is performed by those desiring progeny.

4. **Shrauta Yajñas (Grand Sacrifices):** These are elaborate public ceremonies performed by kings or communities to seek divine blessings for societal welfare. The **Ashvamedha Yajña** and **Rajasuya Yajña** are examples of such grand sacrifices.

The Participants: A Collective Act of Devotion

A Vedic ritual is rarely a solitary act; it is a collective endeavor involving multiple participants, each with a specific role. At the center are the priests, skilled in the intricate art of ritual performance. Their roles are precisely defined: the **Hotr** chants the Rigvedic hymns, the **Adhvaryu** performs the physical acts of the ritual, the **Udgātr** sings the Samavedic melodies, and the **Brahman** oversees the entire process to ensure its correctness.

The yajamāna, or the ritual's sponsor, is an integral participant. The yajamāna represents humanity in its quest for divine connection, offering the fruits of their labor to the cosmos in an act of humble gratitude. The presence of the yajamāna underscores the deeply personal nature of the ritual, reminding us that spirituality is not just a communal endeavor but an individual journey as well.

The Spiritual Significance: Transformation and Liberation

The Vedic rituals are more than acts of devotion; they are profound spiritual practices aimed at transformation and liberation. At their core is the recognition that human existence is intertwined with the cosmos and that true fulfillment lies in aligning oneself with the universal order.

Through the ritual, participants seek to transcend their ego and connect with the greater whole. The offerings symbolize the surrender of material attachments, while the fire represents the transformative power of divine energy. The chanting of mantras elevates the consciousness, creating a bridge between the human mind and the cosmic intelligence.

The ultimate goal of these rituals is **moksha**, or liberation—the realization of one's unity with the infinite. The rituals serve as stepping stones on this path, helping individuals cultivate virtues like humility, discipline, and devotion, which are essential for spiritual growth.

Vedic Rituals in Contemporary Times: A Living Tradition

Even in the modern era, Vedic rituals continue to hold immense significance. While the grand sacrifices of ancient times may have become rare, the principles underlying these rituals remain timeless. Many families and communities still perform daily and seasonal rituals, preserving the essence of Vedic wisdom.

In a world increasingly disconnected from nature, Vedic rituals serve as a reminder of humanity's intimate relationship with the cosmos. They offer a way to reconnect with the sacred, to honor the forces that sustain life, and to find meaning in a world often dominated by material pursuits.

Conclusion: A Timeless Legacy

The Vedic rituals are not merely relics of the past; they are living traditions that embody the highest aspirations of humanity. They teach us to live in harmony with the universe, to approach life with reverence and gratitude, and to seek the divine not as something separate but as an intrinsic part of our being. In their sacred fire, one can glimpse the eternal light of truth, a flame that continues to guide humanity on its journey through time and eternity.

4. Agni as a Cosmic Power

- Role in creation, preservation, and destruction

In the vast expanse of Vedic literature, few entities shine as brightly or as universally as **Agni**, the sacred fire. He is not merely a physical phenomenon or an elemental force; Agni is the very embodiment of cosmic power, a bridge between the mortal and the immortal, the seen and the unseen. As both deity and principle, Agni occupies a central place in the Vedic worldview, weaving through the cycles of creation, preservation, and destruction with divine purpose and energy.

To truly grasp the role of Agni is to embark on a journey that spans the infinite rhythms of existence—an exploration of his transformative essence that shapes not just the physical universe but the spiritual realms as well.

Agni and the Dawn of Creation: The Primordial Spark

In the beginning, when the universe lay shrouded in unmanifest stillness, Agni was the spark that ignited creation. The Vedic hymns describe him as **Hiranyagarbha**, the golden embryo, a glowing seed of cosmic potential nestled within the vast darkness of non-being. The sages envisioned Agni as the first principle of life, a dynamic force that awakened the dormant energies of the cosmos and set them into motion.

The Rigveda, the oldest of the Vedas, celebrates Agni as the **first-born** of existence, the divine flame that emerged from the primordial waters (**apah**) to light the heavens. He is the **hotṛ**, the priest of the gods, who carries the offerings of the creator to the highest realms, ensuring the continuity of existence.

Without Agni, the ṛṣis sang, the universe would remain inert, lifeless, and cold—a realm of potential unrealized.

In the Vedic conception of creation, Agni is not merely the initiator but the sustainer of cosmic processes. He fuels the stars, powers the sun, and breathes vitality into all living beings. Every spark of life, every heartbeat, and every pulse of energy is a manifestation of Agni's presence. As the fire that burns in the belly of the earth and the core of the human soul, he is the driving force behind the evolutionary journey of the cosmos.

Agni the Preserver: The Guardian of Cosmic Order

Once creation is set into motion, Agni assumes the role of preserver, upholding the eternal rhythm of **Ṛta**, the cosmic order. His flames illuminate the paths of existence, guiding both gods and humans toward harmony and balance.

In the physical realm, Agni manifests as the fire that cooks food, providing nourishment and sustenance to all beings. He is present in the hearth of every home, the altar of every temple, and the sun that sustains life on earth. Through his warmth and light, Agni nurtures the cycles of nature—the blooming of flowers, the ripening of fruits, and the transformation of seasons. He is the fire in the forge of the blacksmith and the lamp that illuminates the scholar's desk, enabling the progress of civilization.

In the spiritual realm, Agni plays a central role in the Vedic rituals, acting as the divine mediator between humans and the gods. The **Yajña** (sacrificial fire) is the ultimate symbol of Agni's preserving power. When offerings are made into the sacred fire, it is Agni who consumes them and delivers their essence to the celestial realms. In this act, he not only sustains the bond between mortals and immortals but also preserves the harmony of the universe.

Agni is also the guardian of dharma, the moral law that governs human life. As **Jātavedas**, the knower of all births, he witnesses every thought and action, ensuring that justice is upheld. His flames are both protective and purifying, shielding the righteous while consuming impurities and falsehood.

Agni the Destroyer: The Purifier of the Cosmos

Yet Agni is not merely a force of creation and preservation. His flames are also instruments of destruction, burning away the old to make way for the new. In the cycle of life, death, and rebirth, Agni plays a crucial role as the purifier and transformer.

The destructive aspect of Agni is most vividly seen in the cremation rituals of the Vedic tradition. When a body is offered to the funeral pyre, it is Agni who consumes the physical form and releases the soul from its earthly bonds. This act is not seen as an end but as a passage—a liberation of the soul to continue its journey toward higher realms of existence. In this sense, Agni's destruction is not annihilation but transformation, a necessary step in the eternal cycle of samsara.

In the natural world, Agni's destructive power is equally significant. Forest fires, volcanic eruptions, and lightning strikes are manifestations of his energy, events that clear the old and regenerate the earth. The flames that consume a forest also prepare the soil for new growth, demonstrating Agni's dual role as destroyer and renewer.

Even on the cosmic scale, Agni is envisioned as the force that will eventually dissolve the universe in an act of **Pralaya**, or cosmic dissolution. At the end of the great cycle of time, his flames will consume the heavens and the earth, reducing everything to ash and returning the cosmos to its primordial state. Yet even in this ultimate act of destruction, Agni is not an agent of chaos but a harbinger of renewal, setting the stage for the next cycle of creation.

Agni in the Human Experience: The Inner Flame

Beyond his cosmic roles, Agni is deeply personal, residing within every human being as the **Jatharagni**—the digestive fire that fuels life. In the Vedic view, this inner Agni is a microcosm of the universal flame, linking the individual to the infinite. It is through this fire that we digest not only food but also experiences, emotions, and knowledge.

Agni also represents the fire of aspiration and spiritual yearning. In the Upanishads, he is described as the flame of **tapas**, the inner heat generated through meditation, discipline, and devotion. This spiritual Agni burns away ignorance and impurities, illuminating the path to self-realization. The yogis of ancient India revered this inner flame as the ultimate guide, a divine presence that leads the soul toward liberation.

Agni: The Eternal Flame

The story of Agni is not confined to the myths and hymns of ancient India. It is a story that plays out in every moment of existence, in the crackling of a fire, the warmth of the sun, the glow of a lamp, and the flicker of hope in a human heart. Agni's flames dance through the cycles of creation, preservation, and destruction, reminding us of the eternal nature of existence.

In the light of Agni, the universe finds its rhythm, humanity finds its purpose, and the soul finds its liberation. He is the spark that ignites life, the warmth that sustains it, and the fire that transforms it. To understand Agni is to understand the essence of the cosmos itself—a flame that burns eternally, illuminating the path of existence and beyond.

- Symbolism of fire in Hindu philosophy

Fire, or **Agni**, occupies a central place in Hindu philosophy, not just as an element of the physical world but as a profound symbol of divine energy, spiritual transformation, and the eternal cycles of existence. To the ancient sages of India, fire was not merely a natural force; it was a living, breathing manifestation of the divine, an emissary between the mortal and the immortal realms. Its flickering flames spoke of creation and destruction, purity and passion, light and life. Fire became a universal metaphor for the spiritual journey, a reminder of humanity's connection to the cosmos and its ultimate destiny.

In exploring the symbolism of fire in Hindu philosophy, we delve into a vast tapestry of myths, rituals, and teachings that illuminate its meaning as a source of creation, a purifier, a destroyer, and a bridge to transcendence.

Fire as the Element of Creation: The Divine Spark

The ancient Hindu worldview sees fire as one of the five fundamental elements, or **Panchamahabhutas**, that constitute the universe—alongside earth, water, air, and ether. Among these, fire is considered the most dynamic and transformative. While earth is solid and water flows, fire burns, consumes, and changes everything it touches. This power of transformation makes fire the cornerstone of creation itself.

According to the **Rigveda**, the primordial fire is the source of life, a divine spark that ignited the cosmos from the void of non-being. The hymns celebrate Agni as **Jātaveda**, the one who knows all births, a force that animates the universe and breathes life into all living beings. In this sense, fire represents the creative energy of the cosmos—the vitality that turns potential into form, thought into action, and seed into life.

Every act of creation, whether in nature or in human endeavors, is seen as being fueled by this sacred fire. The sun, often regarded as the celestial embodiment of Agni, is the ultimate life-giver, nurturing the earth with its warmth and light. Similarly, the hearth fire in every home is not merely a source of heat; it is a sacred presence, representing the sustaining power of creation.

Fire as the Purifier: The Flame of Purity

One of the most profound symbolic roles of fire in Hindu philosophy is that of a **purifier**. The searing heat of fire consumes impurities, leaving behind only the essence of what is pure. In the natural world, this is evident in the way fire cleanses by burning away the old and diseased, allowing the new and healthy to emerge.

This purifying power of fire is echoed in Hindu rituals and practices. The **Agni Pariksha**, or "Trial by Fire," is a recurring motif in Indian mythology, symbolizing the testing of truth and virtue. In the epic **Ramayana**, Sita undergoes the Agni Pariksha to prove her purity, stepping into the flames only to emerge unscathed—a testament to her unwavering truth and righteousness.

Fire is also central to Hindu rites of purification. The sacred fire of the **yajna** consumes offerings, transforming them into a spiritual essence that ascends to the divine. Similarly, in cremation, the fire consumes the physical body, purifying the soul and freeing it from earthly attachments so that it may continue its journey toward liberation.

In the human context, fire symbolizes the inner purity of thought, word, and deed. Just as physical fire cleanses the external, the fire of self-discipline, or **tapas**, burns away ignorance and ego, paving the way for spiritual enlightenment.

Fire as the Destroyer: The End and the Beginning

In Hindu philosophy, fire is also a symbol of destruction—a force that reduces everything to ash, dismantling the old to make way for the new. This destructive aspect of fire is not seen as malevolent but as an integral part of the cosmic cycle of creation, preservation, and destruction.

The Hindu trinity of deities—**Brahma** (the creator), **Vishnu** (the preserver), and **Shiva** (the destroyer)—finds its reflection in the symbolism of fire. While fire creates warmth and light, it also consumes and destroys, embodying Shiva's role in dissolving the old to pave the way for regeneration.

The concept of **Pralaya**, or cosmic dissolution, underscores this symbolism. At the end of the cosmic cycle, it is said that the universe will be consumed by fire, returning everything to its primordial state. Yet, this is not an end but a necessary step for a new cycle of creation to begin. Fire, in this sense, is both the destroyer of the old and the womb of the new—a powerful reminder of the impermanence of all things.

In personal terms, fire represents the destruction of ignorance and attachments. The **Bhagavad Gita** often uses the metaphor of fire to describe the transformative power of knowledge. Just as fire consumes fuel, spiritual wisdom burns away the illusions of the material world, leading the seeker toward self-realization.

Fire as the Light of Knowledge: Illuminating the Path

Fire's most enduring symbolic role in Hindu philosophy is as a source of light—a metaphor for knowledge, awareness, and enlightenment. The flickering flame of a lamp, or **Deepa**, represents the light of wisdom that dispels the darkness of ignorance.

The lighting of lamps is a central act in Hindu worship, whether during daily prayers or grand festivals like **Diwali**, the festival of lights. This act is not merely symbolic; it is an invocation of divine wisdom and a reminder of the seeker's ultimate goal—**moksha**, or liberation.

The **Upanishads**, the philosophical texts of Hinduism, frequently draw on the symbolism of fire to describe the spiritual journey. The soul is likened to a flame, and the spiritual path is seen as a process of nurturing and protecting this flame from the winds of distraction and doubt. The ultimate realization, described as merging with the divine, is depicted as the small flame of the individual soul merging with the infinite cosmic fire.

Fire as the Bridge to the Divine: The Sacred Mediator

One of the most unique aspects of fire in Hindu philosophy is its role as a mediator between the human and the divine. In the Vedic tradition, Agni is described as the **priest of the gods**, the one who carries the offerings of humans to the celestial realms. In this role, fire becomes a bridge, connecting the material and spiritual worlds.

In the ritual of **homa** or **havans**, sacred fire acts as the central focus. Offerings of ghee, grains, and herbs are placed into the fire while chanting mantras, with the belief that the flames carry these offerings to the gods. The smoke rising from the fire is seen as a messenger, a visible link between the earthly and the divine.

This symbolic role extends beyond rituals. Fire represents the inner connection between the mortal and the eternal, a reminder that within every human being burns the divine spark of Agni. The journey of life, then, becomes a process of nurturing this spark, transforming it into a radiant flame that illuminates the path to transcendence.

The Eternal Flame: Fire as a Symbol of Life and Liberation

Ultimately, fire in Hindu philosophy is a symbol of life itself. From the fire of digestion that sustains the body to the fire of passion that drives action, from the fire of wisdom that dispels ignorance to the fire of cremation that frees the soul—Agni is present at every stage of existence.

Yet fire is more than a symbol of life; it is a symbol of liberation. The flames remind us of the impermanence of the material world and the eternal nature of the soul. They teach us to burn away our attachments, purify our intentions, and seek the light within.

The journey of fire, from spark to flame to ash, mirrors the journey of the soul—born from the divine, fueled by life, and ultimately returning to its source. In the light of Agni, we see the essence of Hindu philosophy: a celebration of the eternal cycles of creation, preservation, and destruction, and the ever-present possibility of transcendence.

In every flickering flame, the ancient sages saw not just a physical phenomenon but a profound truth—a truth that continues to inspire and illuminate, guiding humanity toward the infinite.

Section 3: Teachings of the Agni Purana

5. Dharma and Ethics

- Guidance on righteous living

In the vast ocean of Hindu scriptures, the **Agni Purana** stands as a luminous guide, shedding light on various aspects of life, spirituality, and morality. Among its most profound teachings is its exposition of **Dharma**—the principle of righteous living—and the ethical codes that govern human life. The Agni Purana does not merely present abstract philosophical concepts; it offers practical wisdom, weaving together the threads of everyday life with the divine tapestry of cosmic order.

This section explores the teachings on **Dharma and Ethics** in the Agni Purana, not as a dry set of rules but as a living philosophy, a story of how human beings can align their lives with the eternal rhythms of the universe.

Dharma: The Cosmic Law

To understand the guidance on righteous living in the Agni Purana, one must first grasp the concept of **Dharma**. In Hindu philosophy, Dharma is more than morality or law; it is the very foundation of existence. The word "Dharma" comes from the Sanskrit root **'dhri'**, meaning "to uphold" or "to sustain." It refers to the principles that uphold the harmony of the universe, ensuring balance between the cosmic, natural, and human realms.

The Agni Purana teaches that Dharma is not a rigid, one-size-fits-all code; it is dynamic and contextual. Dharma varies according to one's **varna** (social role), **ashrama** (stage of life), and individual circumstances. However, the underlying principle remains the same: to live in harmony with truth, justice, and the greater good.

Through its stories, instructions, and dialogues, the Agni Purana paints a vivid picture of Dharma as both a universal law and a personal duty. It reveals that by adhering to Dharma, individuals not only fulfill their worldly responsibilities but also progress toward spiritual liberation.

The Four Pillars of Dharma

The Agni Purana emphasizes that Dharma rests on four foundational pillars, known as the **Purusharthas**, or the goals of human life:

1. **Dharma** (Righteousness): The pursuit of ethical and moral conduct, the foundation of all other goals.

2. **Artha** (Wealth): The acquisition of material prosperity, guided by Dharma.

3. **Kama** (Desire): The fulfillment of desires and pleasures, within the bounds of Dharma.

4. **Moksha** (Liberation): The ultimate goal of life, transcending the material world to attain unity with the divine.

These pillars are not isolated; they are interdependent, with Dharma acting as the guiding force. The Agni Purana teaches that wealth and desire are not inherently bad, but they must be pursued in ways that align with righteous living. Similarly, the path to liberation begins with the foundation of ethical conduct.

Duties of an Individual: The Path of Righteousness

The Agni Purana outlines specific duties and ethical principles for individuals at every stage of life. These duties are presented not as burdens but as opportunities to live a life of purpose and integrity.

1. **For the Householder**: The householder stage, or **Grihastha Ashrama**, is considered the backbone of society. The Agni Purana highlights the duties of householders, including:

   o   Performing daily rituals to honor the gods, ancestors, and sages.

   o   Supporting family members, ensuring their well-being and education.

   o   Engaging in honest labor and sharing wealth with the less fortunate.

   o   Upholding truthfulness, hospitality, and self-restraint.

The Purana reminds householders that their role is not only to sustain their family but to contribute to the greater good of society. Charity, compassion, and adherence to truth are seen as the highest virtues in this stage of life.

2. **For the Renunciate**: For those in the renunciate stage, or **Sannyasa Ashrama**, the Agni Purana teaches detachment and self-discipline. It emphasizes inner purity, meditation, and the

renunciation of material desires. The renunciate is advised to see all beings as equal, transcending ego and selfishness to realize the ultimate truth.

3. **For Kings and Leaders**: The Purana provides detailed guidance on the ethical responsibilities of rulers. A king, or leader, is seen as the protector of Dharma and is tasked with maintaining justice, protecting the weak, and fostering prosperity. The Agni Purana outlines principles of governance, urging rulers to:

   o Rule with compassion and impartiality.

   o Avoid exploitation and uphold justice, even against their own interests.

   o Ensure the welfare of their subjects, prioritizing their needs above personal gain.

Through these teachings, the Purana presents an ideal of leadership based on service, wisdom, and integrity.

The Ethical Code: Ten Cardinal Virtues

The Agni Purana prescribes ten cardinal virtues as the essence of ethical living, applicable to all individuals regardless of their role or stage in life:

1. **Satya (Truthfulness)**: Speaking and living in accordance with truth.

2. **Ahimsa (Non-violence)**: Avoiding harm to any living being, in thought, word, or deed.

3. **Shaucha (Cleanliness)**: Maintaining physical and mental purity.

4. **Daya (Compassion)**: Showing kindness and empathy toward all beings.

5. **Dana (Charity)**: Sharing one's resources with those in need.

6. **Kshama (Forgiveness)**: Letting go of anger and resentment.

7. **Dhairya (Patience)**: Practicing perseverance and tolerance in adversity.

8. **Tapas (Self-discipline)**: Cultivating inner strength through meditation and austerity.

9. **Dhyana (Meditation)**: Seeking clarity and peace through focused contemplation.

10. **Arjava (Simplicity)**: Living with humility and sincerity.

The Purana emphasizes that these virtues are not mere ideals but practical tools for living a balanced and harmonious life.

The Role of Karma and Free Will

The Agni Purana deeply intertwines the concept of Dharma with the law of **Karma**—the principle of cause and effect. It teaches that every action, whether physical, mental, or verbal, creates an imprint on the individual's destiny. Righteous actions aligned with Dharma lead to spiritual growth and liberation, while unrighteous actions result in suffering and bondage.

However, the Purana also highlights the role of **free will**. While Karma shapes the circumstances of one's life, individuals are always free to choose their actions. This freedom is both a responsibility and an opportunity to align oneself with Dharma, transcending the cycles of Karma.

Ethics in Relationships: Harmony with Others

The Agni Purana underscores the importance of ethical behavior in relationships, whether with family, friends, or society at large. It teaches that love respect, and duty form the foundation of all human interactions. Key principles include:

- **Gratitude** toward parents, teachers, and elders, who are seen as embodiments of divinity.

- **Respect** for the sanctity of marriage and the mutual responsibilities of spouses.

- **Kindness** toward all beings, recognizing the interconnectedness of life.

These teachings extend beyond human relationships to include respect for nature and all living creatures, reflecting the Hindu ideal of universal harmony.

The Ultimate Goal: Liberation through Dharma

While the Agni Purana provides detailed guidance for ethical living in the material world, its ultimate focus is spiritual. It teaches that Dharma is not an end in itself but a means to achieve **Moksha**, the liberation of the soul. By living in harmony with Dharma, individuals purify their hearts and minds, paving the way for self-realization and unity with the divine.

A Timeless Message

The teachings on Dharma and Ethics in the Agni Purana resonate across time and space. They offer not just rules but a philosophy of life—one that balances material and spiritual aspirations, personal duties and universal values, individual freedom and cosmic order. In its wisdom, the Agni Purana reminds us that righteousness is not a lofty ideal but a lived reality, a path that every individual can walk to create a life of meaning, harmony, and fulfillment.

Through its luminous teachings, the Agni Purana invites us to kindle the flame of Dharma within our hearts, lighting the way to a life that is not only righteous but divine.

- Laws of karma and cosmic justice

The laws of **karma** are among the most profound and far-reaching concepts in Hindu philosophy. Woven into the very fabric of the universe, karma is both a principle of action and its consequences, a moral law that ensures cosmic justice across the cycles of life, death, and rebirth. The ancient sages believed that no action—be it a fleeting thought, a whispered word, or a bold deed—exists in isolation. Every act creates ripples in the cosmic order, returning to the individual in ways that reflect the true nature of their intentions and choices.

To understand karma is to understand the profound interconnectedness of all things, the balance of cause and effect that sustains the universe. The **Agni Purana**, like many other Hindu scriptures, presents karma not as a punishment or reward, but as an impartial law—a teacher, a guide, and a mirror that reflects the state of one's soul.

This story is an exploration of the laws of karma and cosmic justice, a journey into the heart of a principle that governs not only human life but the very structure of existence.

The Cosmic Weaver: The Origins of Karma

In the beginning, before time and space unfolded, the universe was a vast, silent void. But within this stillness lay potential—a seed waiting to bloom. When creation burst forth, it carried within it the threads of karma, the unseen forces that would weave together the destinies of all beings. This cosmic weaver, impartial and eternal, became the law that bound the actions of individuals to the rhythm of the cosmos.

In Hindu mythology, karma is often linked to the idea of **Rita**, the cosmic order. The Vedas describe Rita as the fundamental principle that ensures harmony and balance in the universe. Karma, as an extension of this order, acts as the mechanism by which balance is maintained. Just as the sun rises and sets, just as the seasons follow their ordained paths, so too does karma ensure that every action finds its rightful consequence.

The Agni Purana teaches that karma is not a punishment decreed by a vengeful god, nor is it a reward bestowed by a benevolent one. Instead, it is an impersonal law, a natural consequence of one's deeds, much like the shadow that follows a body or the echo that answers a call.

Three Types of Karma: The Threads of Destiny

The concept of karma is vast and intricate, encompassing every aspect of human existence. To make sense of its workings, the Agni Purana classifies karma into three distinct types, each representing a thread in the tapestry of destiny:

1. **Sanchita Karma (Accumulated Karma):** This is the sum total of all actions—good and bad—performed by an individual across countless lifetimes. Stored like seeds in the soul's subconscious, these karmas are the dormant causes waiting to bear fruit. Sanchita karma represents the accumulated weight of one's past actions, shaping the potential circumstances of future lives.

The Purana describes this karma as a vast reservoir, an archive of every thought, word, and deed. Some seeds lie dormant for centuries, while others sprout into experiences in the present or future. This karma is not erased but can be transcended through spiritual wisdom and liberation.

2. **Prarabdha Karma (Active Karma):** Prarabdha karma is the portion of accumulated karma that has ripened and is now being experienced in one's current life. It explains the circumstances of one's birth, health, relationships, and challenges. The Agni Purana likens Prarabdha to an arrow already shot—it cannot be recalled or altered. It must run its course, and one must face its consequences with equanimity.

For example, the family one is born into, the physical body one possesses, or the challenges one encounters are manifestations of Prarabdha karma. These are the cards dealt to a person in this life, but how one plays them is governed by free will.

3. **Kriyamana Karma (Future Karma):** Also known as Agami karma, this refers to the actions performed in the present that will shape the future. While one cannot change Prarabdha karma, one has full control over Kriyamana karma. The choices made in the present moment sow the seeds of future experiences, influencing the trajectory of one's soul.

The Agni Purana teaches that Kriyamana karma is a tool of empowerment. By choosing actions aligned with Dharma—righteousness—an individual can create a brighter future and mitigate the effects of past karmas.

Karma and Cosmic Justice: The Eternal Scale

The law of karma is inseparable from the concept of **cosmic justice**, a principle that ensures that every action is met with an appropriate reaction. The Agni Purana presents this justice as a process that unfolds across lifetimes, transcending the limitations of a single existence.

Unlike human justice, which can be swayed by emotions, ignorance, or prejudice, cosmic justice is impartial and exact. It is not bound by time, for the soul's journey is eternal. If an action does not bear fruit in this lifetime, its consequences will manifest in the next or the one after that. The universe never forgets, but it also never punishes arbitrarily. Instead, it mirrors back to the individual the essence of their deeds.

For instance, a person who harms others may not experience suffering immediately, but the seeds of that harm are planted in their karmic field. Eventually, they will face circumstances that reflect the pain they caused, not as punishment but as an opportunity to learn and grow. Similarly, acts of kindness and compassion sow seeds of joy and abundance, creating favorable circumstances in the future.

The Agni Purana explains that this justice is not about reward or retribution but about balance. Every action tilts the cosmic scales, and karma ensures that balance is restored.

The Role of Free Will: The Power of Choice

While karma shapes the circumstances of one's life, it does not negate free will. The Agni Purana emphasizes that every individual has the power to choose their actions, even in the face of challenging karmic circumstances. This freedom is both a responsibility and a gift, allowing individuals to create new patterns and transcend old ones.

For example, a person born into poverty due to past karma is not doomed to suffer indefinitely. Through righteous actions, self-discipline, and spiritual effort, they can transform their circumstances and create a brighter future. Similarly, a person blessed with wealth and privilege is reminded to use their fortune wisely, as their present actions will shape their future karmic account.

The Purana teaches that free will is the key to spiritual growth. By aligning one's actions with Dharma, an individual can rise above the cycles of karma and progress toward **Moksha**, or liberation.

Karma and Rebirth: The Cycle of Samsara

The law of karma is closely tied to the concept of **Samsara**, the cycle of birth, death, and rebirth. The Agni Purana explains that the soul, or **Atman**, is eternal and carries the imprints of karma from one life to the next. Each lifetime is an opportunity to learn, grow, and balance the scales of karma.

The conditions of one's birth—wealth or poverty, health or illness, joy or sorrow—are shaped by the karma of previous lives. However, the ultimate goal is not to accumulate good karma but to transcend the cycle of karma altogether. Liberation, or Moksha, is achieved when the soul breaks free from the bonds of action and realizes its oneness with the divine.

The Role of Dharma in Karma

The Agni Purana highlights the importance of **Dharma**—righteous living—in navigating the complexities of karma. By adhering to ethical principles and fulfilling one's duties with sincerity and selflessness, an individual can create positive karma and avoid actions that lead to suffering.

Dharma serves as a compass, guiding individuals toward actions that align with the greater good. It reminds us that our choices affect not only our own lives but also the lives of others and the balance of the universe.

The Spiritual Path: Transcending Karma

While karma governs the material world, the Agni Purana offers a path to transcendence. Through selfless service, devotion, meditation, and the pursuit of wisdom, one can purify the mind and dissolve the seeds of karma. The ultimate liberation comes when the individual realizes their true nature as the eternal soul, beyond the cycles of action and consequence.

This realization is likened to a fire burning away the accumulated karmic seeds, freeing the soul from the cycle of Samsara. At this stage, the individual acts without attachment, performing their duties with a sense of surrender to the divine.

The Eternal Dance: A Life Guided by Karma

The teachings of the Agni Purana on karma and cosmic justice are a call to mindfulness, compassion, and responsibility. They remind us that every action is significant, every choice a step on the path of spiritual evolution. By understanding the laws of karma, we can navigate life with wisdom and grace, creating a legacy of harmony and balance.

In the flickering flame of karma, we see the reflection of our own lives—a dance of light and shadow, creation and dissolution. And through this dance, the soul journeys toward the ultimate truth, the eternal light of liberation.

6. Knowledge and Sciences

- Astrology, medicine, and architecture

In the golden age of Vedic civilization, knowledge was not compartmentalized into isolated disciplines. Instead, it was seen as a vast, interconnected web—a reflection of the divine order of the cosmos. The **Agni Purana**, one of the ancient scriptures of India, embodies this holistic vision of knowledge. Within its sacred verses, the Purana offers profound insights into the sciences of **astrology**, **medicine**, and **architecture**, presenting them not as mere technical pursuits but as spiritual disciplines deeply rooted in cosmic harmony.

Through the lens of the Agni Purana, these sciences become paths to understanding the universe and humanity's place within it. They bridge the gap between the material and the metaphysical, offering tools for both worldly prosperity and spiritual growth. This story unfolds the deep teachings of the Agni Purana on these three fields, illuminating how ancient wisdom continues to resonate in the modern world.

Astrology: The Dance of the Stars and the Soul

The Agni Purana teaches that the cosmos is a vast, living organism, where every star, planet, and constellation plays a role in the grand symphony of existence. At the heart of this teaching is **Jyotisha**, the science of astrology, which interprets the movements of celestial bodies to reveal the rhythms of human life and destiny.

Astrology, according to the Purana, is not a tool for fortune-telling but a means of understanding the interconnectedness of all things. Just as the moon influences the tides, so too do the planets influence the subtle energies of human existence. The Purana explains that the positions of celestial bodies at the time of one's birth are a reflection of one's **karma**, the accumulated actions of past lives. By studying these patterns, one can gain insight into their life path, challenges, and opportunities.

The Cosmic Map: The Birth Chart

At the core of Vedic astrology is the **Janma Kundali**, or birth chart, a map of the heavens at the moment of one's birth. The Agni Purana describes this chart as a mirror of the soul, revealing:

- The **Lagna** (ascendant), which represents the self and physical body.
- The **Navagrahas** (nine planets), which govern different aspects of life, such as health, relationships, and wealth.

- The **Rashis** (zodiac signs) and **Bhavas** (houses), which provide detailed insights into one's character and destiny.

Through the study of these elements, astrologers can guide individuals in making informed decisions, aligning their actions with the cosmic flow.

Practical Applications of Astrology

The Agni Purana emphasizes the practical use of astrology in daily life. Some key applications include:

1. **Auspicious Timings**: Determining the right moments for important events, such as marriages, business ventures, and spiritual rituals.

2. **Health and Healing**: Understanding how planetary influences affect physical and mental well-being, and using remedies like gemstones, mantras, and rituals to restore balance.

3. **Spiritual Growth**: Identifying one's strengths, weaknesses, and karmic lessons to progress on the path to liberation.

Through these teachings, the Agni Purana reveals astrology as a profound tool for self-discovery and harmony.

Medicine: The Science of Healing and Harmony

In the Agni Purana, the science of **Ayurveda**—the ancient Indian system of medicine—is celebrated as a divine gift for the well-being of humanity. Ayurveda, which translates to "the science of life," is not merely a collection of medical practices but a holistic philosophy that seeks to harmonize the body, mind, and spirit.

The Purana presents medicine as both a practical science and a spiritual discipline. It emphasizes that health is not just the absence of disease but a state of balance where the individual lives in harmony with themselves, society, and nature.

The Three Pillars of Health

According to the Agni Purana, health rests on three foundational principles:

1. **Aahara (Diet):** The Purana underscores the importance of wholesome, sattvic food, tailored to one's constitution. It describes food not only as nourishment for the body but as a source of subtle energy that influences the mind and spirit.

2. **Vihara (Lifestyle):** A balanced routine, including proper sleep, exercise, and meditation, is essential for maintaining health. The Purana advises individuals to live in rhythm with natural cycles, rising with the sun and resting as it sets.

3. **Aushadha (Medicine):** When imbalances occur, the Purana prescribes herbal remedies, therapeutic treatments, and spiritual practices to restore equilibrium.

The Tridosha Theory

At the heart of Ayurvedic medicine is the theory of **Tridosha**, which identifies three primary energies or humors in the body:

1. **Vata (Air and Space):** Governs movement, creativity, and communication.

2. **Pitta (Fire and Water):** Governs digestion, metabolism, and intelligence.

3. **Kapha (Earth and Water):** Governs structure, stability, and immunity.

The Purana explains that each individual has a unique constitution, or **Prakriti**, determined by the balance of these doshas. Health is achieved by maintaining this balance, while imbalances lead to disease. The text offers guidance on recognizing symptoms, diagnosing imbalances, and applying remedies to restore harmony.

Spiritual Healing

Beyond physical treatments, the Agni Purana highlights the importance of spiritual healing. Practices such as mantra chanting, meditation, and rituals are prescribed to cleanse the mind, uplift the spirit, and dissolve karmic patterns that contribute to illness.

Through its teachings on medicine, the Agni Purana reminds us that true healing is holistic, addressing not only the body but the soul's journey toward wholeness.

Architecture: Designing Sacred Spaces

The science of **Vastu Shastra**, or sacred architecture, is another cornerstone of the Agni Purana's teachings. Vastu, which means "dwelling," is the ancient Indian art of designing spaces that align with the forces of nature and the cosmos. According to the Purana, architecture is not just about constructing buildings but about creating environments that support health, prosperity, and spiritual growth.

The Cosmic Blueprint

Vastu Shastra is based on the understanding that the universe is composed of five elements—**earth, water, fire, air, and space**—and that these elements influence human life. The Purana describes how the proper arrangement of these elements in a space can harmonize its energy, promoting well-being and success.

The foundation of Vastu is the **Vastu Purusha Mandala**, a geometric grid that represents the cosmic order. Every building, whether a home, temple, or city, is designed according to this sacred blueprint. Key principles include:

- **Orientation:** Aligning structures with cardinal directions to harness the beneficial energies of the sun, wind, and earth.

- **Proportions:** Using precise measurements and ratios to create harmony between the physical and metaphysical aspects of a space.

- **Zoning:** Allocating specific areas for different activities, such as worship, rest, and work, based on the flow of energy.

Temples as Cosmic Centers

The Agni Purana places special emphasis on temple architecture, describing temples as microcosms of the universe. Every element of a temple, from its foundation to its spire, is symbolic:

- The **Garbhagriha** (sanctum sanctorum) represents the soul, the innermost essence of being.

- The **Shikhara** (tower) symbolizes the ascent to the divine, connecting the earthly and celestial realms.

- The **Mandapa** (hall) serves as a space for communal worship, reflecting the unity of creation.

The Purana also provides guidelines for constructing homes, palaces, and cities, ensuring that all dwellings support the spiritual and material needs of their inhabitants.

The Interconnection of Sciences

The Agni Purana presents astrology, medicine, and architecture not as isolated disciplines but as interconnected paths to understanding the self and the cosmos. Astrology reveals the patterns of destiny, medicine heals the body and mind, and architecture creates environments that support growth and harmony. Together, these sciences reflect the holistic vision of Vedic knowledge, where every pursuit is a step toward aligning with the divine order.

A Legacy for the Ages

The teachings of the Agni Purana on knowledge and sciences are a testament to the profound wisdom of ancient India. They remind us that true knowledge is not about domination or exploitation but about living in harmony with the universe. By integrating these sciences into our lives, we can create a world that is not only prosperous but also aligned with the eternal rhythms of the cosmos.

Through the lens of the Agni Purana, we see knowledge not as an end in itself but as a means to transcendence—a journey from the material to the spiritual, from the finite to the infinite.

- Contributions to cultural and practical wisdom

The **Agni Purana**, one of the most revered texts of ancient India, is not merely a religious scripture; it is a treasure trove of cultural and practical wisdom. Its teachings extend beyond the rituals of devotion to encompass every aspect of human life, offering guidance on how to live with meaning, harmony, and purpose. The Purana serves as a bridge between the spiritual and the worldly, weaving together profound philosophical insights with practical advice for governance, ethics, arts, and daily living.

This is the story of the **Agni Purana's contributions to cultural and practical wisdom**—a narrative of how its timeless teachings have shaped the ethos of Indian civilization and continue to inspire people to this day.

The Purana's Role as a Cultural Compass

In the tapestry of Indian civilization, the Agni Purana is a golden thread, embodying the values, aspirations, and ideals of an ancient society. Its teachings reflect a worldview that recognizes the interconnectedness of all aspects of life, where the material and spiritual realms are not separate but complementary. The Purana offers insights into:

1. **Dharma (Righteousness):** The moral and ethical foundation for individual and societal life.

2. **Artha (Wealth):** The principles of prosperity and governance.

3. **Kama (Desire):** The celebration of beauty, art, and human relationships.

4. **Moksha (Liberation):** The ultimate goal of spiritual enlightenment.

Through these four **Purusharthas**, or aims of life, the Agni Purana provides a holistic framework for living a balanced and meaningful existence.

Practical Wisdom in Governance: The Art of Leadership

The Agni Purana devotes significant attention to the principles of governance and statecraft, offering guidance for rulers and administrators. It emphasizes that a just and prosperous society begins with a wise and virtuous leader. The Purana outlines the qualities of an ideal ruler:

- **Integrity:** A king must be truthful, compassionate, and selfless, putting the welfare of his subjects above his own.

- **Wisdom:** Knowledge of dharma, justice, and the needs of the people is essential.

- **Courage:** The ruler must protect his kingdom with valor and fairness, maintaining peace and order.

The Duties of a King

The Purana advises rulers to:

1. **Uphold Dharma:** The king is seen as the protector of righteousness, ensuring that laws are fair and just.

2. **Promote Prosperity:** By fostering trade, agriculture, and education, the ruler ensures the material well-being of his people.

3. **Defend the Realm:** The Purana emphasizes the importance of a strong military, but only as a means of protecting the innocent and maintaining peace.

4. **Support Culture:** A good ruler is also a patron of the arts, encouraging the growth of literature, music, and architecture.

Through these teachings, the Agni Purana presents governance not as a pursuit of power but as a sacred responsibility.

Cultural Wisdom: The Celebration of Arts and Knowledge

The Agni Purana is a rich repository of cultural wisdom, particularly in the fields of art, literature, and education. It recognizes that culture is the soul of a society, a medium through which values and traditions are preserved and passed on.

Literature and Language

The Purana extols the importance of learning and eloquence, highlighting Sanskrit as the language of the gods. It emphasizes the power of words to inspire, educate, and uplift, encouraging the study of literature, poetry, and philosophy. The text itself is a masterpiece of poetic expression, blending narrative, instruction, and metaphor.

Music and Dance

The Purana celebrates the arts as a means of connecting with the divine. It describes the role of music, dance, and drama in spiritual practice, emphasizing their ability to elevate the soul. Temples often served as centers of cultural activity, where devotional songs and performances brought communities together.

Painting and Sculpture

The Agni Purana provides guidelines for the creation of sacred art, including the proportions and symbolism of idols and murals. These teachings reflect a deep understanding of the psychological and spiritual impact of visual imagery.

The Science of Daily Living: Practical Wisdom for All

The Agni Purana's teachings extend to the minutiae of daily life, offering practical advice on health, hygiene, relationships, and ethics. It recognizes that spirituality is not confined to temples or rituals but is expressed in how one lives each day.

Health and Hygiene

The Purana emphasizes the importance of maintaining physical and mental health as a foundation for spiritual growth. It offers insights into Ayurveda, including:

- The benefits of a balanced diet and regular exercise.
- The use of herbs and natural remedies for common ailments.
- Practices like meditation and pranayama (breathing exercises) to calm the mind and strengthen the body.

Ethics and Relationships

The Agni Purana provides guidance on cultivating harmonious relationships, emphasizing qualities like honesty, kindness, and patience. It underscores the importance of fulfilling one's duties toward family, friends, and society, creating a foundation of trust and respect.

Time Management

The text also advises on the effective use of time, dividing the day into periods for work, rest, and worship. It highlights the value of discipline and routine in achieving personal and spiritual goals.

Architecture and Community Planning

As discussed earlier, the Agni Purana's teachings on **Vastu Shastra** extend beyond individual dwellings to the planning of entire communities. It envisions cities as living organisms, where the placement of buildings, roads, and public spaces reflects the harmony of the cosmos. Key principles include:

- Aligning streets and structures with cardinal directions.

- Creating spaces for worship, education, and commerce.

- Ensuring access to water, greenery, and sunlight.

By integrating spiritual and practical considerations, the Purana offers a blueprint for sustainable and harmonious living.

Karma and Responsibility: The Ethical Framework

Underlying all the Agni Purana's teachings is the concept of **karma**, the law of cause and effect. It emphasizes that every action has consequences, shaping not only the individual's future but also the collective destiny of society. This principle encourages mindfulness, compassion, and responsibility in all aspects of life.

The Purana reminds us that wisdom is not about accumulating knowledge but about applying it in ways that benefit others. It teaches that true success lies not in personal gain but in contributing to the greater good.

A Timeless Legacy

The Agni Purana's contributions to cultural and practical wisdom are a testament to the depth and breadth of ancient Indian thought. Its teachings have influenced countless generations, shaping the values, institutions, and artistic traditions of a civilization that continues to thrive.

Even today, the Purana's wisdom resonates, offering timeless guidance for a world in search of balance and meaning. It reminds us that culture and practicality are not opposites but partners in the dance of life, each enriching the other.

Through its pages, the Agni Purana calls us to live with purpose, creativity, and integrity, honoring the sacred connection between the human spirit and the cosmic order. In its embrace of both the spiritual and the material, it reveals a vision of life that is as inspiring as it is enduring.

7. Spiritual Practices and Devotion

- Rituals, mantras, and yajnas

In the golden age of Vedic India, where every breath was a prayer and every action a sacred offering, the **Agni Purana** emerged as a guiding light for spiritual practices. This revered text, attributed to the divine wisdom of Agni, the fire god, unfolds a universe of profound teachings designed to elevate human consciousness. Central to its teachings are **rituals, mantras, and yajnas**—three timeless tools that serve as bridges between the earthly and the divine. These practices do not merely cater to the individual soul's spiritual awakening; they form the heartbeat of a society harmonized with the cosmic rhythm.

Through the lens of the Agni Purana, rituals are more than tradition, mantras are more than sound, and yajnas are more than fire offerings. Together, they tell the story of humanity's eternal quest to connect with the infinite, weaving a tapestry of devotion, discipline, and divine communion.

Rituals: The Sacred Architecture of Worship

Rituals, or **karmakanda**, are foundational to the Agni Purana's teachings. They are deliberate acts imbued with symbolic meaning, designed to align the individual with the universal. From the simplest daily prayers to elaborate temple ceremonies, rituals are presented in the Purana as acts of both discipline and devotion.

The Purpose of Rituals

In the Agni Purana, rituals serve multiple purposes:

1. **Spiritual Connection**: Rituals are a way to honor and communicate with the divine. They are seen as conversations with the gods, conducted through symbolic actions.

2. **Inner Transformation**: Rituals purify the mind and heart, helping individuals transcend their ego and align with their higher self.

3. **Cosmic Harmony**: By performing rituals, individuals contribute to the balance of the cosmos, acknowledging their role as stewards of creation.

The Purana emphasizes that the true value of a ritual lies not in its complexity but in the **bhava** (intention) behind it. A simple act of lighting a lamp with devotion can be as potent as the most elaborate ceremony.

Types of Rituals

The Agni Purana describes a wide variety of rituals, including:

- **Daily Rites (Nitya Karma):** These include offerings to the sun (Sandhyavandanam), prayers at dawn and dusk, and other personal practices that maintain a connection to the divine.

- **Occasional Rites (Naimittika Karma):** These are performed on special occasions, such as festivals, life milestones, or during times of crisis to seek divine blessings or atonement.

- **Sacramental Rites (Samskaras):** These include rituals that mark the key stages of life, such as birth, initiation, marriage, and death. The Purana provides detailed instructions for these samskaras, ensuring they are performed with sanctity and precision.

Each ritual, no matter how small or grand, is a reminder of the sacredness of life.

Mantras: The Power of Sacred Sound

If rituals are the body of spiritual practice, **mantras** are its soul. The Agni Purana reveres mantras as the primordial sounds that give birth to creation, carrying within them the energy of the cosmos. They are not mere words but vibrations that resonate with the divine frequencies of the universe.

The Essence of Mantras

A mantra is a combination of syllables imbued with spiritual potency. The Purana explains that every mantra has three essential elements:

1. **Sound (Nada):** The vibration of the mantra, which aligns the practitioner's energy with cosmic rhythms.

2. **Meaning (Artha):** The deeper significance or intention behind the mantra, which focuses the practitioner's mind.

3. **Divinity (Devata):** The deity or cosmic power invoked by the mantra.

Mantras are tools for meditation, healing, and spiritual awakening. When chanted with devotion and precision, they unlock hidden energies within the self and the universe.

The Agni Purana's Mantras

The Purana offers numerous mantras for various purposes:

- **Gayatri Mantra**: Revered as the most powerful Vedic mantra, it is a prayer for illumination and wisdom.

- **Beeja Mantras**: These are seed syllables like "Om," "Hrim," and "Shreem," which encapsulate the essence of specific divine energies.

- **Devotional Mantras**: Mantras dedicated to specific deities, such as Vishnu, Shiva, and Durga, are described as paths to divine communion.

The Purana emphasizes the importance of proper pronunciation, rhythm, and mental focus when chanting mantras. It also highlights the transformative power of repetition, or **japa**, which purifies the mind and deepens one's connection to the divine.

Yajnas: The Sacred Fire Offerings

Among all spiritual practices, **yajnas** hold a place of supreme importance in the Agni Purana. A yajna, or fire sacrifice, is described as the highest act of worship, a ritual that nourishes both the earthly and celestial realms. Fire, as Agni, is the medium through which offerings are carried to the gods. It is both a symbol of transformation and a bridge between the mortal and the immortal.

The Philosophy of Yajnas

The Agni Purana presents yajnas as more than mere rituals; they are cosmic acts that sustain the balance of creation. The text teaches that:

- **Agni** is the messenger who carries offerings to the gods and brings their blessings to humanity.

- **Offerings (Ahutis)** symbolize the surrender of ego and desires, transforming material elements into spiritual energy.

- **Harmony** is achieved when yajnas are performed with devotion, aligning human actions with divine will.

Yajnas are not confined to physical fire ceremonies. The Purana also speaks of **inner yajnas**, where the fire is the spiritual energy within, and the offerings are thoughts, emotions, and actions.

Types of Yajnas

The Agni Purana describes various types of yajnas, each serving a unique purpose:

1. **Shrauta Yajnas:** Performed according to Vedic injunctions, these include grand sacrifices like the Ashvamedha (horse sacrifice) and Rajasuya (royal consecration).

2. **Grihya Yajnas:** Domestic rituals conducted for personal and family well-being, such as the Agnihotra (daily fire offering).

3. **Special Yajnas:** Performed for specific goals, such as invoking rain, ensuring fertility, or seeking peace during times of conflict.

Each yajna is a communal act, often involving the participation of priests, family members, and the community. The Purana emphasizes that the merit of a yajna is multiplied when performed selflessly and with the welfare of all beings in mind.

The Inner Meaning of Spiritual Practices

Beyond their outward forms, the Agni Purana reveals the deeper, symbolic meanings of rituals, mantras, and yajnas:

- **Rituals** represent the alignment of human actions with the cosmic order.

- **Mantras** symbolize the power of sound and intention to shape reality.

- **Yajnas** embody the principle of self-sacrifice, reminding us that true growth comes from giving rather than taking.

These practices are not ends in themselves but tools for self-transformation. They help individuals transcend their limitations, awaken their inner divinity, and realize their unity with the cosmos.

The Eternal Flame of Devotion

Through its teachings on spiritual practices, the Agni Purana kindles the eternal flame of devotion in the hearts of its readers. It reminds us that spirituality is not a distant ideal but a living reality, expressed in the simplest acts of love and reverence.

Whether through the precision of a ritual, the resonance of a mantra, or the transformative power of a yajna, the Purana offers pathways to the divine that are as relevant today as they were thousands of years ago. It invites us to see the sacred in the everyday, to light the fire of devotion within, and to walk the path of dharma with faith and joy.

In its embrace of rituals, mantras, and yajnas, the Agni Purana tells a story of connection—between the individual and the infinite, the seen and the unseen, the transient and the eternal. It is a story that continues to inspire, illuminating the path to spiritual awakening for generations to come.

- Path to liberation through fire worship

In the quietude of ancient forests and on the banks of mighty rivers, where sages once meditated in the glow of flickering flames, a profound spiritual tradition was born. This was the path of **fire worship**, a sacred practice where the purifying flames of Agni became a bridge to the ultimate goal of existence: **moksha**, or liberation from the cycle of birth and death. The story of this path, as revealed in the **Agni Purana** and other sacred texts, is one of transformation, surrender, and unity with the divine.

Through the lens of fire worship, the journey to liberation unfolds as a symphony of rituals, mantras, and yajnas, all centered around the eternal flame that resides both in the outer world and within the depths of the human soul. This is the story of how fire becomes not just a symbol, but a living force guiding the seeker from ignorance to enlightenment.

The Sacred Flame: Fire as a Gateway to the Divine

To understand the path to liberation through fire worship, one must first grasp the significance of **Agni**, the Vedic fire god. In the cosmic narrative of creation, Agni is the first spark, the primordial energy that transforms the unmanifest into the manifest. He is the messenger of the gods, the purifier of all things, and the sustainer of life.

But Agni is more than an external force. In the teachings of the Agni Purana, fire is both a **cosmic power** and a **personal guide**:

- **As the Cosmic Flame:** Agni is the divine energy that pervades the universe, present in the sun, stars, and lightning.

- **As the Inner Fire:** Agni resides in every being as the spark of consciousness, the energy of digestion (jatharagni), and the spiritual flame that fuels devotion.

This dual nature of Agni makes fire worship a profound spiritual practice. By honoring the external fire, the seeker awakens the inner fire, setting the stage for self-realization.

The Ritual of Fire Worship: A Sacred Offering

The foundation of fire worship lies in the ritual of the **yajna**, the sacred fire offering. In a yajna, fire is kindled and offerings such as ghee, grains, and herbs are poured into the flames while chanting mantras. On the surface, it appears as a simple act of devotion. But the Agni Purana reveals a deeper symbolism:

1. **Fire as the Divine Mediator:** When offerings are placed in the fire, they are transformed into smoke and energy, ascending to the heavens. Agni, as the divine messenger, carries these offerings to the gods, ensuring a connection between the mortal and the immortal.

2. **Purification and Transformation:** Just as fire consumes impurities, the ritual purifies the practitioner's mind and soul. It symbolizes the burning away of desires, ego, and attachments that bind one to the material world.

3. **Sacrifice and Surrender:** The act of offering represents the surrender of the self. By giving up material possessions and inner attachments to the fire, the seeker aligns with the cosmic principle of selflessness.

Each yajna is a microcosm of the spiritual journey, where the fire becomes a guide, teacher, and purifier.

Mantras: The Voice of the Flame

In fire worship, **mantras** play a central role. These sacred sounds, when chanted during yajnas, invoke divine energies and focus the mind. The Agni Purana emphasizes that the power of fire is amplified through the resonance of mantras.

One of the most revered mantras in fire worship is the **Gayatri Mantra**, dedicated to the sun, the ultimate source of light and energy:

"Om Bhur Bhuvah Swah,
Tat Savitur Varenyam,
Bhargo Devasya Dheemahi,
Dhiyo Yonah Prachodayat."

This mantra is a prayer for illumination, seeking the light of wisdom to dispel the darkness of ignorance. When chanted before the sacred fire, it creates a powerful synergy, aligning the seeker's inner flame with the cosmic light.

Other mantras invoke specific deities associated with fire, such as Agni, Surya (the sun god), and Rudra (a fierce form of Shiva). These mantras are not mere words but vibrations that resonate with the energy of the flames, creating a bridge to higher consciousness.

The Inner Yajna: Awakening the Fire Within

While external fire worship is a profound practice, the Agni Purana also speaks of an **inner yajna**, a spiritual process that takes place within the seeker. Here, the fire is not a physical flame but the inner **jatharagni**, the spiritual fire of awareness.

The Fire of Awareness

The inner yajna involves offering thoughts, desires, and emotions into the fire of consciousness. This practice is a form of meditation, where the seeker observes and dissolves the ego and attachments. The Agni Purana teaches that:

- The **fuel** for the inner fire is devotion and discipline.
- The **offerings** are negative traits such as anger, greed, and ignorance.
- The **result** is clarity, purity, and the awakening of the soul's true nature.

This inner yajna transforms the seeker, leading to a state of **vairagya** (detachment) and **jnana** (wisdom), essential steps on the path to liberation.

The Final Liberation: Moksha Through Fire

The culmination of fire worship is **moksha**, the liberation of the soul from the cycle of birth and death. The Agni Purana describes moksha as the merging of the individual flame with the universal fire. This union is achieved through:

1. **Self-Purification:** Just as fire burns away impurities, the spiritual journey removes the layers of ignorance and ego that obscure the soul's true nature.

2. **Surrender to the Divine:** Through rituals and inner yajnas, the seeker learns to let go of attachments and align with the will of the cosmos.

3. **Realization of Oneness:** In the final stage, the seeker recognizes that the inner flame and the cosmic fire are one and the same. This realization brings liberation.

Even in death, fire plays a sacred role. In Hindu tradition, the body is cremated, and the flames release the soul from its physical vessel. This act symbolizes the soul's journey toward the ultimate light.

A Legacy of Light

The path to liberation through fire worship is not just a spiritual practice; it is a way of life. It teaches the seeker to live with awareness, humility, and reverence for the divine forces that sustain existence. The Agni Purana's teachings on fire worship reveal a timeless truth: that within the heart of every being burns an eternal flame, a spark of the divine waiting to unite with its source.

As the story of fire worship unfolds, it becomes clear that Agni is not just a god of fire but a guide on the spiritual journey, leading the soul from darkness to light, from ignorance to wisdom, and ultimately, from bondage to liberation.

In the glow of the sacred flame, the seeker finds not only the path but the destination—a journey that begins and ends in light.

Section 4: Mythology and Stories

8. Legends of Agni

- Stories of Agni's manifestations

In the tapestry of Vedic mythology, where gods and mortals intertwined in timeless sagas, one figure burns brightly across all tales — **Agni**, the god of fire. He is no ordinary deity, for he embodies both the physical and metaphysical aspects of existence. Agni is the fire that warms the hearth, the flame that purifies offerings, and the cosmic energy that fuels creation, sustains life, and transforms it into ash for renewal. His stories, woven into the fabric of the **Vedas, Puranas**, and epics, reveal his many forms and manifestations, each a chapter in the grand narrative of life and the cosmos.

Through these tales, Agni emerges not merely as a natural force but as a living, breathing entity—both a guide and a witness to the journey of humanity and divinity alike. Let us now step into the world of his legends, where flames flicker with mystery, power, and divine purpose.

The Birth of Agni: Fire as the Firstborn of Creation

In the beginning, when the universe lay shrouded in darkness and silence, the gods convened to bring forth the elements of creation. According to the **Rig Veda**, Agni was the first to emerge, born of the friction between the celestial parents, **Dyaus (the sky)** and **Prithvi (the earth)**. His birth was marked by a divine spark, a tiny flame that quickly grew to illuminate the cosmos.

Agni's origin is layered with symbolic depth. He is described as the **child of the heavens and earth**, the bridge between the mortal and the divine. The gods entrusted him with the sacred task of carrying offerings to the celestial realms, making him the eternal messenger between humans and gods. This role gave him the title **"Havyavahana"**, the carrier of sacrificial offerings.

In another myth, Agni is said to have been hidden by his mother, Earth, fearing his insatiable hunger might consume the world. The gods searched tirelessly for him, and when they finally found him concealed in water and vegetation, they praised his power and boundless energy. This tale highlights Agni's omnipresence — he resides in the warmth of the sun, the flicker of lightning, the spark of life, and the glow of consciousness within all beings.

Agni's Manifestations: The Triple Flame

The **Rig Veda** speaks of Agni's triadic nature, describing him as the fire on earth, the lightning in the sky, and the sun in the heavens. These three forms symbolize his all-encompassing presence in the universe:

1. **Agni as Bhumi (Earthly Fire):** He is the fire kindled in yajnas (sacrificial rituals), the flame that cooks food, and the warmth that sustains life.

2. **Agni as Vidyut (Lightning):** He is the spark of storms, the celestial fire that tears through the sky, and the harbinger of rain, which nourishes the earth.

3. **Agni as Surya (Solar Fire):** He is the energy of the sun, the eternal flame that governs the cycles of day and night and sustains all creation.

Each manifestation serves a purpose, reflecting Agni's role as both a nurturer and a destroyer. His triple form also signifies the three realms of existence — the mortal, the celestial, and the divine — uniting them in a cosmic harmony.

The Tale of Svaha: Agni and His Eternal Hunger

One of the most well-known stories of Agni involves **Svaha**, his devoted consort and embodiment of sacrificial offerings. According to the **Mahabharata**, Agni's hunger was insatiable, and he consumed offerings at an alarming rate. The gods, worried that his voracious appetite might disturb the balance of creation, sought a way to temper him.

Svaha, a radiant goddess, approached Agni and offered herself to him. She explained that she would act as the intermediary for all sacrifices, ensuring that Agni received his share without overwhelming the world. In gratitude, Agni accepted her as his eternal consort, and their union symbolized the harmonious balance between fire and sacrifice.

Through this story, the mythology conveys an essential truth: while Agni represents power and transformation, he also requires regulation and guidance, embodied by Svaha. Their partnership teaches that raw energy, when tempered by wisdom and devotion, becomes a force for creation rather than destruction.

The Legend of Agni and the Khandava Forest

One of the most dramatic episodes involving Agni occurs in the **Mahabharata**, during the burning of the **Khandava Forest**. This tale is a vivid illustration of Agni's destructive yet purifying nature.

Agni, weakened by overconsumption of impure offerings, approached **Krishna** and **Arjuna**, seeking their help to regain his strength. He explained that consuming the medicinal herbs and flora of the Khandava Forest would rejuvenate him, but the forest was protected by **Indra**, the king of the gods, who would not allow its destruction.

With Krishna as his strategist and Arjuna as his warrior, Agni took the form of an all-consuming fire and descended upon the forest. The flames devoured everything in their path, but this destruction was not aimless—it was a renewal, paving the way for new life. The story underscores the dual role of Agni as both destroyer and creator, illustrating the cycle of destruction and regeneration that governs the universe.

The Curse and Redemption of Agni

In another tale, Agni finds himself cursed for his actions. According to the **Brahmanas**, Agni once refused to consume a sinful offering, arguing that it would taint his purity. The gods, angered by his defiance, cursed him to consume everything indiscriminately, whether pure or impure.

Burdened by the curse, Agni grew despondent. He wandered the heavens and earth, lamenting his fate. It was then that the gods, realizing the importance of Agni's purity, offered him redemption. They decreed that while Agni must consume all offerings, his flames would purify them, transforming even the impure into sacred energy.

This story reveals Agni's role as a purifier and reconciler. He teaches that even in the presence of impurity, transformation is possible through the fire of self-discipline and devotion.

Agni as a Teacher and Guide

Agni is not only a god of rituals and energy but also a teacher of spiritual truths. In the **Kathopanishad**, he appears as a guide to **Nachiketa**, a young seeker who wishes to understand the mystery of death and immortality. Agni teaches Nachiketa the secrets of the sacred fire and the path to moksha, emphasizing the importance of self-sacrifice, discipline, and devotion.

This narrative highlights Agni's role as a spiritual guide, illuminating the path to liberation for those who seek wisdom.

The Eternal Flame: Agni in Every Heart

The legends of Agni culminate in a profound truth: that the flame he represents is not confined to the external world but burns within every being. The Agni Purana teaches that the inner flame, or **jatharagni**, is the source of life, consciousness, and spiritual awakening. To honor Agni is to honor the divine light within oneself, nurturing it through knowledge, devotion, and righteous action.

Through his many manifestations—whether as the fire of sacrifice, the flame of destruction, or the inner light of wisdom—Agni reveals the interconnectedness of all existence. His stories remind us that fire is both a physical and spiritual force, a bridge between the material and the eternal.

Agni, the eternal flame, continues to burn in the myths, rituals, and hearts of those who seek his light, guiding humanity on its timeless journey toward truth and liberation.

- Episodes from the Mahabharata and Ramayana

The **Mahabharata** and the **Ramayana**, two of the greatest epics of ancient India, are vast oceans of stories interwoven with deep spiritual, ethical, and philosophical insights. In these epics, the figure of **Agni**, the god of fire, plays pivotal roles, often as a transformative force—both literal and symbolic. His presence in the narratives transcends the physical, representing purification, renewal, divine will, and the eternal interplay of creation and destruction.

Let us dive into the luminous episodes of Agni's intervention in these timeless epics, where his flames illuminate moments of profound significance, catalyzing the destinies of gods and mortals alike.

Agni's Role in the Mahabharata

The Burning of the Khandava Forest

Among Agni's most celebrated episodes in the Mahabharata is his role in the **burning of the Khandava Forest**, a tale that intertwines destruction with divine purpose.

The Backdrop: Agni's Hunger

The story begins with Agni, the celestial fire, lamenting his weakened state. Over centuries, Agni had consumed innumerable offerings during rituals, but the impurities of these sacrifices had dulled his brilliance and vitality. To regain his strength, Agni approached **Brahma**, the Creator, seeking advice. Brahma revealed that consuming the abundant medicinal herbs and life forms of the **Khandava Forest** would restore Agni's energy. However, this forest was under the protection of **Indra**, the king of gods, who would not allow its destruction because his friend **Takshaka**, the serpent king, resided there.

Determined, Agni sought allies who could help him overcome Indra's resistance. It was then that he encountered the legendary heroes **Krishna** and **Arjuna**, who were wandering near the forest. Agni approached them in the guise of an old man and revealed his plight. He implored their assistance, promising them celestial weapons in return.

The Battle of Flames and Storms

Moved by Agni's plea, Krishna and Arjuna agreed to help. To aid them in the battle, Agni invoked **Varuna**, the god of oceans, who gifted Arjuna the **Gandiva bow**, an indestructible weapon, along with an inexhaustible quiver of arrows. Krishna wielded his celestial discus, the **Sudarshana Chakra**, which could cut through anything in its path.

When Agni ignited the forest with his fiery form, Indra descended in rage, summoning torrential rains to extinguish the flames. What followed was an epic battle:

- Arjuna, standing like a colossus, shot arrows that formed a protective canopy, preventing the rain from reaching the forest.
- Krishna, with his Sudarshana Chakra, neutralized Indra's storms, allowing Agni to consume the forest unhindered.

Despite Indra's resistance, the flames engulfed the Khandava Forest. Many beings perished, but some, like **Maya**, the celestial architect, were spared due to Krishna's mercy. In gratitude, Maya later built the magnificent **Maya Sabha**, the royal hall of the Pandavas in Indraprastha.

Symbolism and Lessons

The burning of the Khandava Forest is not merely an act of destruction but a profound allegory for transformation. The forest, teeming with life, represents the human ego and attachments. Agni's flames symbolize purification, the necessary destruction of the old to make way for renewal. Through this tale, the Mahabharata conveys that destruction, when aligned with divine will, paves the way for greater creation and evolution.

The Birth of Draupadi and Dhrishtadyumna

Another tale where Agni's role is central is the **birth of Draupadi**, the heroine of the Mahabharata, and her brother **Dhrishtadyumna**, the warrior prince destined to slay Drona.

The story begins with **King Drupada**, ruler of Panchala, who seeks revenge against **Drona**, his childhood friend turned enemy. To achieve this, Drupada performs a great yajna, invoking Agni with intense devotion. As the flames rise high, Agni manifests from the sacrificial fire, carrying within him two divine beings:

- **Dhrishtadyumna**, a warrior destined to kill Drona.

- **Draupadi**, a radiant maiden who would become the wife of the Pandavas and a key figure in their destiny.

Agni's involvement in this tale underscores his role as a divine agent of karma, bringing forth beings to fulfill cosmic justice. The fire not only symbolizes transformation but also the divine will that shapes the threads of fate.

Agni's Role in the Ramayana

The Trial by Fire: Sita's Agni Pariksha

One of the most poignant episodes involving Agni in the Ramayana is **Sita's Agni Pariksha**, the trial by fire. This event occurs after Lord Rama rescues Sita from the clutches of Ravana, the demon king of Lanka.

The Doubt and the Ordeal

Despite his unwavering love for Sita, Rama feels compelled to address the doubts of his subjects regarding her purity after her time in Ravana's captivity. To prove her chastity and silence critics, Sita voluntarily undergoes a trial by fire.

In a deeply emotional moment, Sita steps into a blazing pyre, invoking Agni to bear witness to her truth. The flames, instead of consuming her, part around her like a protective cocoon. Agni himself appears, radiant and resplendent, and declares Sita pure and untouched.

Symbolism of the Trial

The Agni Pariksha is layered with symbolism:

1. **Purity and Truth:** Fire, as a purifier, tests and reveals the truth. Sita's unscathed emergence from the flames signifies the triumph of truth and virtue over doubt and slander.

2. **Devotion and Surrender:** By stepping into the fire, Sita exemplifies absolute faith in divine justice, surrendering herself to the cosmic order.

3. **The Dual Nature of Fire:** Agni is both a destroyer and a protector. While he has the power to consume, he also safeguards those who are righteous and pure.

This episode highlights Agni's role as a divine witness and arbiter of truth, reinforcing the idea that fire is not just a physical element but a moral force in the universe.

Agni and the Birth of Rama's Sons

Another significant moment involving Agni occurs at the end of the Ramayana, when Sita, abandoned by Rama, seeks refuge in the ashram of **Valmiki**, the sage who composed the epic. While residing there, she gives birth to Rama's twin sons, **Lava** and **Kusha**.

According to certain versions of the Ramayana, these children are seen as divine gifts of Agni, born through his blessings. Agni's presence in their story reinforces the themes of renewal and the continuity of dharma, ensuring that the legacy of Rama and Sita endures.

Agni as the Eternal Witness

In both epics, Agni's manifestations serve as a reminder of his omnipresence and multifaceted role in the cosmic order. Whether he acts as a purifier, a protector, or a destroyer, Agni is always aligned with the principles of **dharma** and cosmic justice. His flames illuminate paths of transformation, where ego, doubt, and ignorance are burned away to reveal truth, virtue, and renewal.

Through the Mahabharata and the Ramayana, Agni's stories remind us that fire is not merely a physical force but a divine energy that shapes the destinies of gods and mortals alike. His flames are both gentle and fierce, nurturing creation while ensuring that the balance of the universe is preserved. As the eternal flame, Agni stands as a beacon of truth, guiding humanity through the cycles of destruction and rebirth toward the ultimate realization of dharma and cosmic harmony.

9. Mythical Narratives in Agni Purana

- Tales of gods, sages, and kings

The *Agni Purana*, one of the eighteen *Mahapuranas*, is a treasure trove of mythology, spiritual wisdom, and ethical guidance. Rooted in the rich traditions of Hindu cosmology, it presents a tapestry of tales that blend cosmic truths with earthly realities. The narratives encompass the exploits of gods, the trials of sages, and the legacies of mighty kings. These stories, timeless in essence, serve as profound allegories for moral dilemmas, human struggles, and divine interventions.

The Origin of Creation: The Primordial Tale

At the heart of the *Agni Purana* lies the grand narrative of creation. In the beginning, there was nothing but the eternal void. From this void emerged Brahman, the ultimate reality, who manifested as Lord Brahma, the creator. With his immense willpower (*iccha-shakti*), Brahma gave rise to the cosmos. The tale describes how Brahma, seated on a lotus that sprouted from the navel of Lord Vishnu, began the act of creation by invoking the power of *tapas* (austerity).

From his mind were born the *manasputras*—the sages Marichi, Atri, Angiras, Pulastya, Pulaha, Kratu, and Vashistha. These sages became the architects of the universe, responsible for the spread of wisdom and dharma. The narrative vividly describes the emergence of the first elements—earth, water, fire, air, and ether—and their amalgamation to form the tangible world. This tale symbolizes the interconnectedness of all existence and the divine orchestration behind creation.

The Churning of the Ocean: A Cosmic Struggle

One of the most captivating stories in the *Agni Purana* is the tale of the *Samudra Manthan*, the churning of the ocean. This epic event was a collaboration between the devas (gods) and asuras (demons) to obtain the nectar of immortality (*amrita*). Mount Mandara was used as the churning rod, while the serpent Vasuki served as the rope. Lord Vishnu, in his *Kurma* (tortoise) avatar, supported the mountain on his back, preventing it from sinking.

As the churning progressed, various celestial objects emerged from the ocean, including the moon, the goddess Lakshmi, the divine horse Uchchaihshravas, and the deadly poison *Halahala*. It was Lord Shiva who consumed the poison to save the world, his throat turning blue as a result, earning him the name *Neelkanth*.

This tale illustrates the eternal struggle between good and evil, the cooperation required for great endeavors, and the sacrifices made by the divine for the welfare of creation.

The Tale of Sage Parashurama: The Warrior Ascetic

The *Agni Purana* recounts the life of Parashurama, the sixth avatar of Vishnu, born to Sage Jamadagni and Renuka. A fiery ascetic and an unparalleled warrior, Parashurama's story is one of vengeance, redemption, and the preservation of dharma.

When the tyrannical Kshatriya king Kartavirya Arjuna killed Parashurama's father over a divine cow, the sage took up arms to avenge the injustice. Wielding his mighty axe, he waged a campaign to rid the world of corrupt kings, cleansing the earth of oppression 21 times.

Yet, his tale is not just one of wrath but also of immense spiritual depth. After fulfilling his mission, Parashurama retreated into asceticism, relinquishing his weapons and dedicating himself to meditation. His story underscores the balance between action and renunciation, reminding humanity of the need to align personal duty (*svadharma*) with universal justice (*sanatana dharma*).

The Legend of King Harishchandra: The Pinnacle of Truth

Among the many royal tales, the story of King Harishchandra stands out as an epitome of truth and virtue. Harishchandra, a descendant of the solar dynasty, was renowned for his unwavering commitment to truth. The Purana narrates how the sage Vishwamitra tested his resolve by subjecting him to relentless trials.

Forced to relinquish his kingdom, wealth, and family, Harishchandra endured unimaginable hardships. He served as a cremation ground attendant, performing the most menial of tasks. Despite his suffering, he remained steadfast in his adherence to truth. His story culminates in divine intervention, as the gods restore his kingdom and bless him for his unyielding righteousness.

Harishchandra's tale is a poignant reminder of the power of integrity and the ultimate triumph of virtue over adversity.

The Sage Agastya: Balancer of the Cosmos

The *Agni Purana* gives prominence to Sage Agastya, whose deeds shaped the cosmic and terrestrial realms. Born of the gods Mitra and Varuna, Agastya played a pivotal role in restoring balance in creation.

One tale recounts how Agastya consumed the ocean to reveal the demons hiding within, enabling the devas to defeat them. Another story describes how he subdued the Vindhya mountains, which were growing so tall that they obstructed the sun's path. Through humility and wisdom, Agastya persuaded the mountains to bow and never rise again, ensuring the natural order.

His journey to the south, where he spread Vedic knowledge and established dharma, symbolizes the dissemination of spiritual wisdom across geographical and cultural boundaries.

The Birth of Skanda: The God of War

The birth of Skanda (Kartikeya), the god of war, is a tale of divine strategy narrated in the *Agni Purana*. When the asura Tarakasura gained immense power through a boon, only a son of Shiva could defeat him. The gods conspired to unite Shiva and Parvati, resulting in the birth of Skanda.

Raised by the celestial nymphs, the *Krittikas*, Skanda grew into a formidable warrior. Leading the divine armies, he vanquished Tarakasura and restored balance to the heavens. This story is an allegory of the triumph of divine will and collective effort over tyranny.

The Cosmic Dance of Shiva: The Tandava

The *Agni Purana* vividly describes Lord Shiva's *Tandava*, the cosmic dance of creation and destruction. This dance, performed in a moment of divine ecstasy, signifies the eternal cycle of birth, preservation, and dissolution.

The Purana narrates how Shiva's dance annihilates the universe at the end of each cosmic cycle, paving the way for renewal. Accompanied by the rhythmic beats of the *damaru* and the flames of his third eye, the dance is both a spectacle of destruction and a promise of regeneration.

The *Tandava* embodies the transient nature of existence and the ultimate reality of transformation.

These mythical narratives from the *Agni Purana* are not mere stories but profound lessons woven into the fabric of Hindu thought. They transcend time and space, offering insights into the human condition and the divine mysteries of the universe. As they unravel the deeds of gods, sages, and kings, they invite readers to embark on a journey of self-discovery and spiritual awakening.

- Moral lessons and symbolic meanings

The *Agni Purana* is not merely a compilation of myths and rituals; it is a repository of profound moral lessons and symbolic meanings. Beneath the layers of epic tales and cosmic events lies an intricate web of teachings designed to guide humanity in its journey toward righteousness (*dharma*), self-awareness, and spiritual enlightenment. Each story serves as a mirror, reflecting human dilemmas and divine solutions, urging readers to seek higher truths while navigating the complexities of existence.

The Eternal Struggle Between Good and Evil: The Churning of the Ocean

The story of the *Samudra Manthan* (churning of the ocean) is one of the most symbolic narratives in the *Agni Purana*. On the surface, it is an epic saga of gods and demons uniting to obtain the nectar of immortality (*amrita*). Yet, the tale holds deeper moral and symbolic significance.

The ocean represents the human mind, vast and filled with hidden treasures and dangers. The churning is symbolic of introspection and spiritual effort, where the forces of good (devas) and evil (asuras) within every individual clash in the quest for higher truth. The appearance of *Halahala*, the deadly poison, signifies the obstacles and challenges one must face during self-discovery. Lord Shiva's act of consuming the poison symbolizes the need for sacrifice and selflessness to protect others and ensure progress.

The ultimate emergence of *amrita* reminds us that perseverance and cooperation, even among opposing forces, can lead to the realization of divine grace. The lesson is clear: life's struggles and inner conflicts are necessary for personal growth and the attainment of spiritual nectar.

The Unyielding Power of Truth: The Story of Harishchandra

The tale of King Harishchandra exemplifies the invincibility of truth (*satya*) and righteousness (*dharma*). Faced with relentless trials imposed by Sage Vishwamitra, Harishchandra loses his kingdom, wealth, and family, descending into a life of abject poverty. Despite the enormity of his suffering, he remains unwavering in his commitment to truth.

The symbolic meaning of his trials reflects the inevitable hardships faced by those who choose the path of truth. His willingness to perform the lowly duties of a cremation ground attendant, while adhering to his principles, teaches the value of humility and service.

Harishchandra's ultimate restoration by divine intervention highlights that while truth may lead to temporary hardships, it is ultimately rewarded with eternal glory. The lesson resonates deeply: truth is not just a moral virtue but a divine force that upholds the cosmos.

The Balance of Action and Renunciation: The Tale of Parashurama

The story of Parashurama, the warrior sage, illustrates the delicate balance between action (*karma*) and renunciation (*sannyasa*). Parashurama's wrathful annihilation of the Kshatriya rulers, undertaken to cleanse the earth of tyranny, symbolizes the righteous use of power to restore order. However, his subsequent renunciation of arms reflects the need to relinquish worldly attachments once justice is restored.

This duality teaches that while action is essential for the fulfillment of duty (*dharma*), true liberation lies in detachment and self-realization. The symbolism of his axe, used to eliminate injustice, further underscores the importance of wielding power responsibly and only in alignment with divine principles.

Parashurama's tale reminds us that life requires both engagement in the world and a readiness to step away when the time for reflection and spiritual growth arises.

The Cosmic Balance: The Story of Agastya

Sage Agastya's role in balancing the cosmos carries profound symbolic meanings. When the Vindhya mountains grew so tall that they obstructed the sun's path, Agastya humbly approached them and requested them to bow until his return, thereby restoring cosmic harmony. This act symbolizes the power of humility and wisdom in overcoming insurmountable challenges.

Similarly, Agastya drinking the ocean to expose the demons hiding within illustrates the power of inner strength and resolve in confronting negativity. The ocean represents the subconscious mind, and the hidden demons symbolize latent fears and desires. Agastya's act reminds us of the need to face our inner darkness with courage and determination to achieve spiritual clarity.

Through these narratives, the *Agni Purana* emphasizes that balance—in nature, society, and the self—is essential for harmony and progress.

The Symbolism of Lord Shiva's Tandava

Lord Shiva's *Tandava*, as described in the *Agni Purana*, is a cosmic dance of creation, preservation, and destruction. This dance is not merely a physical act but a profound symbol of the eternal cycles of the universe. Each step and gesture of the *Tandava* carries deep meaning.

The flames in Shiva's hand represent destruction, a necessary precursor to creation. His *damaru* (drum) signifies the rhythm of life, the vibrations that sustain existence. The raised hand in *abhaya mudra* offers protection and reassurance, symbolizing Shiva's role as a compassionate guardian amidst chaos.

The *Tandava* teaches that destruction is not an end but a transformation—a way for the old to make way for the new. It urges us to embrace change, understanding that life's impermanence is part of the divine plan.

The Birth of Skanda: Triumph of Divine Will

The story of Skanda, born to defeat the demon Tarakasura, symbolizes the power of divine will and collective effort. Skanda's birth was not an ordinary event but the result of the gods pooling their energies to manifest a savior. His upbringing by the *Krittikas* represents the nurturing of divine potential by earthly forces.

Skanda's victory over Tarakasura signifies the triumph of righteousness over chaos. It reminds us that divine intervention often works through human and cosmic collaboration. His youthful vigor and leadership also inspire us to face challenges with courage, confidence, and purpose.

The Unity of Opposites: The Story of Shiva and Parvati

The relationship between Shiva and Parvati, as recounted in the *Agni Purana*, is a profound allegory for the union of opposites. Shiva, the ascetic, and Parvati, the embodiment of fertility and life, represent the balance between renunciation and engagement. Their union gives birth to cosmic harmony and reflects the idea that creation is possible only through the integration of contrasting forces.

This narrative teaches the importance of embracing diversity and finding unity in duality. It also underscores the idea that spiritual growth requires both inner stillness and active participation in life.

Conclusion: The Timeless Relevance of the *Agni Purana*

The moral lessons and symbolic meanings in the *Agni Purana* transcend time and culture, offering universal truths applicable to all aspects of life. Through its vivid stories, the Purana urges us to uphold truth, embrace balance, act with righteousness, and seek the divine within ourselves. It serves as both a spiritual guide and a mirror, reflecting the eternal dance of cosmic forces and the profound journey of the human soul.

Each tale is a call to introspection, urging readers to uncover the deeper truths hidden beneath the surface of myths, and to apply these lessons in their pursuit of a life aligned with dharma and self-realization.

Section 5: Agni's Eternal Relevance

10. Symbolism of Agni in Modern Times

- Fire as a metaphor for knowledge and transformation

Agni, the eternal flame of the Vedas, is not confined to ancient rituals or sacred chants; its essence transcends time, embodying profound truths that remain deeply relevant in modern life. The symbolic fire, once worshipped as the cosmic mediator between humans and the divine, has evolved into a metaphor for knowledge, transformation, and the undying human spirit. In the flickering glow of Agni, we find the story of progress, enlightenment, and the unyielding desire for change.

The Fire of Knowledge

Imagine a solitary flame, steady yet alive with movement. It illuminates the darkest corners, revealing hidden truths and banishing ignorance. This is the symbolic role of Agni as the fire of knowledge (*jnana-agni*). Just as fire transforms raw matter into something refined, knowledge transforms the human mind, burning away falsehood and misunderstanding to reveal the brilliance of truth.

In modern times, this fire manifests in the relentless pursuit of education, innovation, and exploration. Every scientific discovery, every technological breakthrough, every artistic masterpiece is a spark of Agni—an embodiment of the light of human intellect. When a student spends sleepless nights poring over books, the flame of their lamp mirrors the inner fire of curiosity and determination.

Agni teaches us that knowledge is not static; it is dynamic, ever-evolving. It urges us to question, explore, and ignite our minds. But, like physical fire, knowledge must be wielded with responsibility. Misused, it can scorch and destroy; properly harnessed, it can illuminate and uplift humanity.

The Fire of Transformation

Fire is a force of transformation. It melts, forges, and reshapes. In the physical world, it turns raw ore into gleaming metal, food into nourishment, and waste into ash. Symbolically, Agni represents the transformative power that drives personal and societal evolution.

Consider the trials of life—the losses, failures, and hardships that feel like consuming flames. These moments of pain are not mere destruction but a process of refinement. The fire of suffering burns away ego, pride, and attachment, leaving behind a stronger, purer self. This transformative fire is akin to the process of forging steel: the raw material must endure intense heat to emerge resilient and unbreakable.

In the modern world, this symbolism finds expression in the stories of individuals who rise from adversity. A person who rebuilds their life after loss, a community that thrives after calamity, or a nation that transforms through struggle—all carry within them the essence of Agni. Transformation is rarely easy, but it is essential for growth.

Agni's transformative power also speaks to the broader cycles of change. From environmental shifts to social revolutions, the fire of transformation continues to shape the world. Protests, movements, and reforms—all are modern manifestations of Agni, burning away outdated systems to make way for progress.

Agni as a Catalyst for Inner Growth

On a personal level, Agni symbolizes the inner fire of willpower and determination. In the ancient Vedic rites, fire was kindled through friction—a process that mirrors the human struggle to ignite one's inner strength. Agni teaches us that growth often comes from friction, from the challenges that test our resilience.

In modern life, this fire takes the form of ambition and self-discipline. A runner pushing through exhaustion, an entrepreneur persevering through setbacks, or an artist perfecting their craft—all embody the flame of Agni. This inner fire is not just about achieving goals but about refining the self, burning away laziness, fear, and doubt to reveal one's true potential.

The Fire of Unity and Connection

In ancient rituals, Agni was the bridge between humans and the divine, carrying offerings to the heavens and blessings back to earth. In modern times, fire retains its symbolic role as a unifying force. Around a campfire, strangers share stories and become friends. During celebrations, fireworks light up the night sky, bringing communities together. Even in times of loss, the sacred flame of a funeral pyre unites families in remembrance.

Agni reminds us of the power of connection. Just as fire requires fuel, oxygen, and heat to burn, human relationships thrive on mutual effort, trust, and shared warmth. In a world increasingly divided by borders and ideologies, the symbolism of Agni as a force of unity is more relevant than ever.

The Dual Nature of Fire: Creation and Destruction

Agni's dual nature—as both creator and destroyer—mirrors the complexities of modern life. Fire, when controlled, is a source of light and warmth, but when unleashed, it becomes a force of devastation. This duality is a powerful metaphor for the tools and technologies of the modern age.

Consider nuclear energy: it can power cities or annihilate them. The internet connects billions but also spreads misinformation. Artificial intelligence holds the promise of revolutionizing industries but raises ethical dilemmas. Agni teaches us to approach such dualities with wisdom, balancing creation and destruction, harnessing fire for the greater good while preventing it from consuming us.

Agni and the Quest for Spiritual Enlightenment

Beyond its physical and societal symbolism, Agni represents the spiritual fire that burns within every soul. This fire, known as *tapas*, is the heat of austerity, meditation, and devotion. In the chaos of modern life, where distractions abound, this inner flame is a beacon of focus and clarity.

Meditation, yoga, and spiritual practices are the modern kindling for this fire. They help individuals burn away the clutter of the mind, revealing the pure light of awareness. Agni's relevance lies in its reminder that amidst the noise of the world, the most important fire is the one that burns quietly within, guiding us toward self-realization.

Conclusion: Agni's Timeless Flame

Agni, the sacred fire, continues to burn brightly in the modern world, not as a relic of the past but as a living symbol of knowledge, transformation, and unity. It reminds us that within every challenge lies the potential for growth, within every moment of darkness lies the promise of light, and within every individual lies the power to ignite change.

In the glowing embers of a fireplace, the flicker of a candle, or the sparks of inspiration, Agni lives on, whispering ancient truths to a modern world. It is a call to embrace the flame within, to let it illuminate our paths, transform our lives, and connect us to the eternal rhythm of existence.

- Relevance in contemporary spiritual practices

In the heart of every ancient tradition, there lies a core that transcends time—a timeless flame that continues to illuminate the path for humanity. Agni, the sacred fire, is one such eternal essence. Though its physical presence in Vedic rituals may seem distant to modern lives, its spirit is alive, deeply embedded in contemporary spiritual practices. From meditation halls to yoga studios, from temples to quiet spaces of reflection, Agni's relevance burns brightly, shaping spiritual journeys in profound ways.

The Ever-Burning Flame: Agni in Meditation and Yoga

In the stillness of meditation, one often visualizes a flame—a steady, unyielding light at the center of one's being. This visualization is not coincidental. It is Agni, the inner fire, symbolizing awareness and concentration. Just as a flame consumes impurities, meditation burns away distractions, anxieties, and attachments, revealing the clarity of the self.

Modern practitioners of yoga and mindfulness often speak of the *agni* within—the metaphorical fire housed in the solar plexus, called the *manipura chakra*. In yoga, this inner fire is cultivated through practices like *pranayama* (breath control) and *asana* (physical postures). The fiery energy of Agni is said to fuel transformation, both physical and spiritual, helping practitioners purify their bodies and minds.

In the dynamic movements of *Surya Namaskar* (Sun Salutation), Agni is invoked to awaken vitality and energy. Every stretch, every controlled breath, feeds the inner flame, connecting the practitioner to the cosmos. Agni, as the ancient sages understood, is not just external; it is the force that sustains life, guiding individuals toward harmony and enlightenment.

Agni in Rituals of Renewal

The ancient practice of kindling sacred fire during rituals may no longer dominate contemporary households, yet the essence of these rituals persists in subtle ways. Lighting a candle before meditation or prayer, igniting incense to create a sacred atmosphere, or even the simple act of sitting by a fireplace for contemplation—all echo the ancient reverence for Agni.

In modern spiritual communities, the fire ceremony (*havan* or *homam*) remains a cherished practice. Gathered around the sacred flames, individuals offer prayers, chanting ancient mantras that invoke transformation and cleansing. The fire consumes physical offerings, symbolizing the burning away of negativity and ego. Even in this digital age, these ceremonies remind practitioners of the transformative power of surrender and purification, teaching that to grow, one must let go.

Agni as the Guide in Inner Alchemy

The fire of Agni is not limited to external rituals; it serves as a metaphor for the inner alchemical process—the transformation of the soul. In modern spiritual practices like *tantra* and *kundalini yoga*, Agni is the spark that ignites spiritual awakening.

The rising *kundalini* energy, often described as a coiled serpent at the base of the spine, is awakened through focused practice and devotion. As it ascends through the body's energy centers, it encounters the fire of the *manipura chakra*, which propels it upward, burning away the veils of ignorance. This journey, deeply rooted in ancient Vedic symbolism, continues to inspire seekers today, offering a roadmap for personal transformation and self-discovery.

Agni and the Art of Letting Go

Fire's ability to consume and transform makes it a powerful symbol for release—a lesson that resonates deeply in modern spiritual practices. Letting go of the past, surrendering fears, and burning away attachments are central themes in personal growth and healing.

Consider the symbolic act of burning letters, papers, or mementos associated with pain. This modern ritual, though seemingly unrelated to ancient Vedic practices, is an echo of Agni's role as the purifier. In spiritual retreats and workshops, participants often engage in fire ceremonies where they write down their burdens and release them into the flames, watching as Agni transforms their pain into ash, clearing the way for renewal.

Agni in Community and Connection

In a world often fragmented by technology and isolation, the fire remains a symbol of unity. Modern spiritual gatherings frequently use fire as a focal point for connection. Whether it's a group meditation by candlelight, a communal fire ceremony, or even a casual bonfire, Agni brings people together, fostering a sense of shared purpose and belonging.

Fire circles, popular in many contemporary spiritual traditions, embody the ancient wisdom of Agni as a bridge between the individual and the collective. Participants gather around a central flame, sharing stories, singing, or simply sitting in silence, drawing strength from the fire's warmth and light. These moments of communion are reminders that while the paths of seekers may differ, the essence of Agni unites all.

The Inner Fire of Purpose

In today's fast-paced, achievement-driven world, spiritual practices often emphasize reconnecting with one's purpose—a concept deeply tied to Agni. The fire within is not just a source of energy; it is the beacon that guides one's life. This inner fire is what drives passion, creativity, and the courage to pursue one's dharma, or life's calling.

Modern self-help philosophies and spiritual teachings frequently draw upon this metaphor, encouraging individuals to "find their spark" or "ignite their passion." These phrases, though contemporary, are rooted in Agni's eternal symbolism. They remind us that the flame within is the source of all creation and the key to a fulfilling life.

Agni in the Age of Sustainability

Even in the context of environmental consciousness, Agni retains its relevance. Fire, as a force of both creation and destruction, serves as a reminder of balance and responsibility. Contemporary spiritual practices often emphasize living in harmony with nature, and Agni's dual nature mirrors this balance.

The sacred fires of the past were never wasteful; they were offerings made with reverence and understanding of nature's cycles. Today, this philosophy inspires eco-conscious practices in spiritual communities, encouraging mindful consumption and sustainable living. Agni teaches that while fire can nourish, it must be respected, reminding us of our duty to preserve the delicate equilibrium of life.

Conclusion: Agni's Guiding Light

Agni, the eternal flame, continues to illuminate the modern seeker's journey, bridging the ancient and the contemporary. Its symbolism as a purifier, transformer, and unifier is woven into the fabric of spiritual practices worldwide. Whether through meditation, rituals, or personal growth, Agni burns as a constant reminder of the divine potential within each of us.

In its glow, we find wisdom, transformation, and connection—a timeless flame guiding humanity toward light, clarity, and transcendence. Agni's relevance is not confined to the past; it is the fire that fuels the future, inviting every seeker to kindle their inner flame and embrace the eternal dance of creation and renewal.

11. Agni Purana's Influence

- Impact on Hindu rituals, art, and philosophy

The *Agni Purana*, a treasure trove of spiritual wisdom and practical knowledge, has radiated its influence far beyond its textual confines. Revered as a guiding scripture, its teachings have left indelible marks on Hindu rituals, art, and philosophy. As a compendium that seamlessly bridges the sacred and the worldly, it has shaped not only how Hindus worship but also how they view existence, express creativity, and seek enlightenment. Its influence is as vast as the fire it venerates—burning brightly through generations, inspiring tradition, and igniting transformation.

Agni Purana and the Ritualistic Fabric of Hinduism

The *Agni Purana* is unparalleled in its detailed instructions on *yajnas* (fire sacrifices), *pujas* (worship rituals), and the conduct of spiritual ceremonies. Agni, the sacred fire, stands as the central figure in these rites, symbolizing the bridge between humans and the divine. The *Agni Purana* doesn't merely describe the rituals—it breathes life into them, embedding profound symbolism and purpose into every act of worship.

In households across India, the morning ritual of lighting a lamp owes its origins to the principles detailed in the *Agni Purana*. The lamp's flame, considered a manifestation of Agni, purifies the surroundings, dispels darkness, and invites divine blessings. While this act may appear simple, its roots lie in the ancient understanding that fire is both a purifier and a transmitter of prayers to the gods.

The Purana's emphasis on *homas*—the ceremonial offering of ghee, grains, and other sacred items into the fire—has made these rituals cornerstones of Hindu life. Whether it's a wedding, a housewarming ceremony, or the consecration of a temple, the *homa* is an invocation of Agni as a witness and a conduit of divine grace. The *Agni Purana* meticulously outlines the chants, offerings, and protocols for these ceremonies, ensuring that the sacred flame is honored as the essence of divine presence.

Art and Architecture: Agni's Creative Inspiration

The *Agni Purana* also delves deeply into *shilpa shastra*—the ancient science of art and architecture. Its influence is evident in the magnificent temples of India, where every pillar, carving, and mural echoes the scripture's teachings. The Purana's guidance on proportions, symbolism, and iconography has shaped how sacred spaces are conceived and constructed.

In temple architecture, the sanctum sanctorum (*garbhagriha*) is often compared to the womb of creation, with Agni as the life-giving spark at its core. The towering *vimanas* (temple spires) are designed to resemble the flame of Agni, reaching upward toward the heavens. This architectural symbolism draws directly from the *Agni Purana's* teachings, reminding devotees that the temple is not just a physical structure but a living embodiment of cosmic principles.

Agni's influence extends to sculpture and painting as well. The Purana provides precise descriptions of deities, emphasizing the interplay of form and essence. Agni is often depicted with fiery hair, a radiant complexion, and multiple arms holding sacred implements—an image that symbolizes his transformative and all-encompassing power. These depictions, inspired by the *Agni Purana*, have become enduring motifs in Hindu art, shaping how generations visualize the divine.

Philosophical Illumination: Agni as a Cosmic Principle

The *Agni Purana* is not merely a manual for rituals; it is a profound exploration of philosophical truths. Its teachings elevate Agni from a physical element to a cosmic principle, embodying creation, sustenance, and dissolution. This triadic nature of Agni parallels the Hindu concept of the Trimurti—Brahma, Vishnu, and Shiva—making Agni a central figure in understanding the cycles of existence.

In the *Agni Purana*, Agni is described as the eternal witness, the force that resides within every being as *jatharagni* (digestive fire), *pranagni* (vital energy), and *jnanagni* (the fire of knowledge). This understanding has deeply influenced Hindu philosophy, where fire becomes a metaphor for self-purification and spiritual growth.

The Purana's philosophical teachings resonate in the Bhagavad Gita, where Lord Krishna speaks of offering all actions into the fire of yoga. This concept, rooted in the *Agni Purana*, emphasizes the idea that life itself is a sacred offering, a perpetual *yajna* where every thought, word, and deed is consumed by the fire of divine purpose.

Agni Purana's Ethical and Moral Compass

The *Agni Purana* is as much a guide for ethical living as it is a repository of rituals. Its teachings on dharma (righteousness) have profoundly influenced Hindu ethics, offering practical advice on relationships, governance, and personal conduct. Agni, as the eternal witness, becomes a symbol of accountability, urging individuals to act with integrity and self-awareness.

Kings and rulers in ancient India often turned to the *Agni Purana* for guidance on just governance. Its emphasis on fairness, compassion, and the welfare of all subjects shaped the political ethos of the time, inspiring leaders to rule as servants of dharma rather than as wielders of power.

In contemporary times, the Purana's moral teachings remain relevant, reminding individuals of the importance of living in harmony with nature, respecting others, and seeking balance in life. Its lessons transcend the boundaries of religion, offering universal principles that resonate with seekers of truth.

The Eternal Flame: Agni Purana's Legacy

The *Agni Purana's* influence is as vast as it is profound. Its teachings continue to shape the spiritual, artistic, and philosophical landscape of Hinduism, ensuring that the sacred flame it venerates never fades. From the flickering lamp in a devotee's home to the towering spires of temples, from the depths of meditation to the heights of artistic expression, Agni's presence is felt everywhere, a timeless reminder of the divine spark within all creation.

Through its rituals, art, and philosophy, the *Agni Purana* teaches that fire is more than an element—it is a symbol of transformation, a source of inspiration, and a guide to the eternal. Its legacy endures, burning brightly in the hearts of those who seek light, truth, and transcendence.

- Legacy in shaping cultural traditions

The *Agni Purana* is not merely a text; it is a living legacy, woven into the intricate tapestry of India's cultural traditions. Its profound teachings and narratives have left an enduring mark on how Hindus celebrate life, honor divinity, and understand their place in the cosmos. This influence extends beyond the spiritual domain, touching every aspect of culture—festivals, family customs, societal norms, and the arts. Like the sacred fire it venerates, the *Agni Purana* has illuminated the path of cultural evolution, its warmth and light enduring across millennia.

Festivals as Embodiments of Agni's Teachings

The vibrant festivals of India owe much of their grandeur and symbolic depth to the teachings of the *Agni Purana*. Agni, the sacred fire, is central to these celebrations, symbolizing purity, transformation, and the divine connection. The Purana not only provides detailed descriptions of rituals but also imbues these traditions with philosophical meaning, ensuring that every act of celebration becomes an act of devotion.

One of the most prominent examples is the festival of *Diwali*, the Festival of Lights. While it is celebrated across India for various reasons—Lord Rama's return to Ayodhya, the victory of Goddess Lakshmi, or the triumph of good over evil—it is the lighting of lamps that unites all these narratives. This act, rooted in the teachings of the *Agni Purana*, symbolizes the victory of knowledge over ignorance and the dispelling of darkness from the soul. Every flickering lamp is a tribute to Agni, the eternal flame that guides humanity toward enlightenment.

Similarly, the festival of *Lohri* in northern India celebrates the agricultural cycle, with offerings made to the sacred fire as a gesture of gratitude. The *Agni Purana's* emphasis on fire as the receiver of offerings and the bearer of blessings has shaped this practice, making Agni not just a deity but an inseparable part of cultural life. Whether it's *Holika Dahan*—the burning of the effigy to signify the destruction of evil—or the fire rituals during Navratri, the Purana's influence is unmistakable.

Family Customs and the Flame of Tradition

In Hindu households, the teachings of the *Agni Purana* manifest in daily life through customs and traditions centered around fire. The practice of lighting a *diya* (oil lamp) at dawn and dusk is a direct invocation of Agni's presence, believed to purify the home and invite auspicious energies. This simple act, guided by the Purana, is a reminder of Agni's role as a purifier and protector, ensuring that the sacred flame of tradition burns brightly in every household.

Marriage ceremonies, one of the most significant rites of passage, are deeply influenced by the *Agni Purana*. The *saptapadi*—the seven sacred steps taken by the couple around the fire—derives its sanctity from the text's teachings. Agni is invoked as a witness to the vows, symbolizing the eternal bond between the couple and their commitment to dharma. The fire is not merely a ritualistic element; it is a silent observer, a divine force that sanctifies the union.

Even in moments of farewell, the *Agni Purana* provides guidance. The cremation rites, where the body is offered to Agni, reflect the belief that fire serves as the bridge between the earthly and the divine. This practice is a testament to the Purana's profound impact on cultural traditions, ensuring that Agni accompanies individuals through every stage of life.

Societal Norms and Ethical Foundations

The *Agni Purana* extends its influence to societal norms, embedding its teachings in the ethical fabric of communities. Agni, as the eternal witness, symbolizes accountability and righteousness, principles that have shaped social conduct and relationships. The Purana's emphasis on truth, fairness, and self-discipline has inspired a culture that values integrity and justice.

In the ancient system of justice, Agni was often invoked in oaths and trials. The belief that fire could reveal the truth reflects the *Agni Purana's* teachings on Agni as a purifier and protector of dharma. This reverence for Agni's role as a moral arbiter continues in modern traditions, where honesty and responsibility are upheld as sacred virtues.

The Purana's guidance on hospitality, charity, and compassion has also influenced societal norms. The act of offering food to guests, known as *atithi devo bhava* (the guest is God), reflects Agni's role as the divine receiver of offerings. This practice, rooted in the Purana, has fostered a culture of generosity and mutual respect, making hospitality a cornerstone of Indian life.

Cultural Expressions Through Art and Literature

The teachings of the *Agni Purana* have inspired countless expressions of creativity, shaping the arts and literature of India. The Purana's vivid descriptions of Agni's attributes, along with its rich repository of myths and allegories, have provided artists with a timeless source of inspiration. Paintings, sculptures, and temple carvings often depict Agni in his divine form, with flaming hair and radiant energy, embodying his transformative power.

In classical dance forms like *Bharatanatyam* and *Kathakali*, the symbolism of fire is often represented through movements and gestures. The dancers, embodying Agni's energy, tell stories of creation, destruction, and renewal, bringing the teachings of the *Agni Purana* to life. Similarly, classical music compositions often draw upon the Purana's themes, using metaphors of fire to convey emotions and spiritual truths.

The Purana's influence extends to literature as well, inspiring poets and writers to explore themes of transformation and divine connection. From ancient epics to modern interpretations, the *Agni Purana's* legacy is a guiding flame, illuminating the path for storytellers across generations.

The Eternal Flame of Cultural Legacy

The *Agni Purana* is more than a scripture; it is a cultural cornerstone, a flame that has lit the way for generations. Its teachings, rooted in the sanctity of Agni, have shaped how Hindus live, celebrate, and express their connection to the divine. Whether in the sacred rituals of a temple, the joyful celebrations of a festival, or the quiet sanctity of a family home, the *Agni Purana's* influence is ever-present, a reminder that fire is not just an element—it is life itself.

In shaping cultural traditions, the *Agni Purana* has ensured that the sacred fire it venerates burns eternally, connecting the past, present, and future in a timeless dance of light and devotion. It is a legacy that transcends time, inspiring humanity to seek truth, uphold dharma, and honor the divine spark within all creation.

Conclusion

• Summarizing the eternal wisdom of the Agni Purana

The *Agni Purana* stands as a timeless beacon of spiritual, cultural, and philosophical wisdom, embodying the transformative power of Agni—the sacred fire. Its teachings transcend the boundaries of time, offering guidance for individual growth, societal harmony, and cosmic understanding. Rooted in the principles of dharma, the text emphasizes truth, purity, and devotion as the pathways to divine realization.

Through its intricate tales of gods, sages, and kings, the *Agni Purana* reveals profound moral lessons, blending myth with meaning. It bridges the sacred and the mundane, making its teachings accessible in rituals, art, and daily life. The Purana reminds us that Agni is not merely a deity but a symbol of inner light, knowledge, and transformation—a force that purifies, sustains, and connects.

Even in modern times, the *Agni Purana* retains its relevance, guiding humanity toward ethical living, spiritual fulfillment, and harmony with the natural world. Its enduring legacy, etched into cultural traditions and philosophical frameworks, serves as a testament to its universal and eternal wisdom.

As the sacred flame of Agni continues to burn, the *Agni Purana* invites us to kindle the fire within—awakening our highest potential and embracing the eternal truths that unite us with the divine.

• The flame of knowledge as a guiding light for humanity

The *Agni Purana* elevates fire—Agni—not just as an element of nature but as the eternal flame of knowledge, illuminating the path for humanity. This sacred flame symbolizes wisdom, self-awareness, and the power to transcend ignorance. It teaches that, like fire, knowledge has the ability to transform, purify, and renew, igniting the spark of divinity within every soul.

In the Purana's verses, Agni serves as a mediator between the mortal and the divine, bridging the physical and the spiritual. Similarly, knowledge is portrayed as the ultimate tool to connect humanity with higher truths, guiding individuals to live with purpose and align with dharma. Agni's flame reminds us that, through learning and self-discovery, we can overcome darkness and create a life of clarity and meaning.

Even in today's world, the teachings of the *Agni Purana* endure. Fire remains a metaphor for intellectual curiosity and spiritual enlightenment, urging humanity to seek wisdom that uplifts and unites. Just as a single flame can light countless others without diminishing, the flame of knowledge, once kindled, becomes an eternal source of light for all.

Through its timeless wisdom, the *Agni Purana* inspires us to nurture this inner flame, allowing it to guide our thoughts, actions, and aspirations. In doing so, it affirms that the pursuit of knowledge is not just a journey—it is the sacred light that illuminates humanity's collective path to truth and transcendence.

Appendices

• Key Sanskrit verses with translations

1. ## यज्ञो वै श्रेष्ठतमं कर्म।
   (Yajño vai śreṣṭhatamaṁ karma)
   Translation: "Sacrifice is the highest form of action."

   ○ This verse emphasizes the significance of selfless actions and offerings, symbolizing the purification of the soul through devotion and duty.

2. ## अग्निर्देवो द्विजातीनां।
   (Agnir devo dvijātīnāṁ)
   Translation: "Agni is the deity of the twice-born (the learned and enlightened)."

   ○ It highlights Agni as the divine medium for wisdom, purity, and spiritual progress, central to rituals and sacred rites.

3. ## अग्निना रयिमश्नवत्।
   (Agninā rayimaśnavat)
   Translation: "Through Agni, one attains prosperity."

- o This verse underscores Agni as a symbol of abundance, prosperity, and the fulfillment of righteous desires.

4. **ज्ञानं शुद्धमग्निस्वरूपम्।**
(Jñānaṁ śuddham agnisvarūpam)
Translation: "Pure knowledge is the essence of fire."

   - o It compares the illuminating power of knowledge to the purifying and transformative nature of fire.

5. **अग्निः सर्वभूतानां हृदि स्थितः।**
(Agniḥ sarvabhūtānāṁ hṛdi sthitaḥ)
Translation: "Agni resides in the hearts of all beings."

   - o This verse conveys the universal presence of Agni, symbolizing inner light and consciousness.

6. **धर्मो रक्षति रक्षितः।**
(Dharmo rakṣati rakṣitaḥ)
Translation: "Dharma protects those who uphold it."

   - o It emphasizes the protective and sustaining power of righteousness, an overarching theme in the *Agni Purana*.

7. **अग्निः पावकः पवित्रकः।**
(Agniḥ pāvakaḥ pavitrakaḥ)
Translation: "Agni is pure and the purifier."

   - o This verse extols Agni's purifying role in rituals and spiritual practices.

8. **विद्या ददाति विनयं।**
(Vidyā dadāti vinayaṁ)
Translation: "Knowledge bestows humility."

   - o It reflects the transformative power of knowledge, aligning with Agni's role as a harbinger of enlightenment.

9. **अग्निहोत्रं परं धर्मः।**
(Agnihotraṁ paraṁ dharmaḥ)
Translation: "The fire sacrifice is the supreme dharma."

   - o This verse elevates sacrificial offerings as the highest form of devotion and moral duty.

10. **सर्वं ज्ञानप्लवेनैव वृजिनं संतरिष्यसि।**
(Sarvaṁ jñānaplavenaiva vṛjinaṁ saṁtariṣyasi)
Translation: "Through the boat of knowledge, one crosses all obstacles."

   - o It symbolizes knowledge as a liberating force, akin to Agni's power to destroy impurities and illuminate the path to salvation.

- Glossary of terms and concepts

1. **Agni**: The Vedic fire god, symbolizing purity, transformation, and the bridge between the human and the divine. Agni is central to rituals and spiritual practices in Hinduism.

2. **Agnihotra**: A sacred fire ritual performed at sunrise and sunset, symbolizing offerings to Agni and the cycle of life and renewal.

3. **Dharma**: The cosmic law and moral order that governs the universe and human life, often translated as righteousness or duty.

4. **Yajna**: A Vedic ritual involving offerings to deities through the sacred fire, representing selfless acts of devotion and the interconnectedness of all life.

5. **Pavaka**: A name for Agni, meaning "the purifier," emphasizing fire's role in cleansing impurities both physically and spiritually.

6. **Purana**: Ancient Hindu texts that narrate mythological, historical, and philosophical stories, often offering moral and spiritual guidance.

7. **Jñana**: Knowledge or wisdom, often regarded as the key to spiritual enlightenment and liberation from ignorance.

8. **Diksa**: A spiritual initiation or consecration process in Hinduism, often involving fire rituals to mark the beginning of a devotee's journey on the spiritual path.

9. **Samskara**: Rites of passage in Hindu culture, marking significant stages in an individual's life, often performed with Agni as a witness.

10. **Upasana**: Devotional worship or meditation aimed at connecting with the divine, often involving offerings to the sacred fire.

11. **Svaha**: A sacred exclamation uttered during fire offerings, symbolizing the act of surrendering to the divine.

12. **Homa**: A fire ritual in which offerings are made to deities, seeking blessings, purification, and prosperity.

13. **Tattva**: Fundamental principles or elements of creation in Hindu philosophy, often associated with the five classical elements: earth, water, fire, air, and ether.

14. **Prana**: The vital life force or energy that flows through all living beings, often linked metaphorically to the sustaining power of fire.

15. **Rta**: The cosmic order and truth that sustains the universe, upheld through the practice of dharma and yajna.

16. **Shakti**: The divine feminine energy, often associated with creation and transformation, paralleling the dynamic nature of fire.

17. **Tapas**: Austerity or disciplined spiritual practice, often linked with the heat or energy generated by self-discipline and devotion.

18. **Vedanga**: The six auxiliary disciplines of the Vedas, including rituals, phonetics, and astrology, integral to understanding sacred texts like the *Agni Purana*.

19. **Ahuti**: Offerings made into the sacred fire during rituals, symbolizing devotion and surrender to the divine.

20. **Kundalini**: Spiritual energy believed to reside at the base of the spine, often described as a coiled serpent, activated through sp ritual practices and likened to the transformative power of fire.

This glossary provides clarity on key terms and concepts from the *Agni Purana*, enriching the reader's understanding of its teachings.

- Bibliography for further study

1. **Agni Purana** (translated by various scholars)

   o This core text is essential for a deeper understanding of the content, structure, and teachings of the *Agni Purana*. Available in various translations and commentaries, each offering unique insights into its symbolic, mythological, and ritualistic aspects.

2. **The Bhagavad Gita** (translated by Eknath Easwaran)

   o A key scripture in Hindu philosophy, exploring the paths of karma, bhakti, and jñana, with many parallels to the moral and spiritual teachings found in the *Agni Purana*.

3. **The Vedas** (translated by Swami Sivananda, Max Muller, and others)

   o As the source of many concepts in the *Agni Purana*, the Vedas, particularly the Rigveda, contain hymns and invocations that detail the role of Agni as a primordial deity and cosmic principle.

4. **Purāṇic Encyclopedia** by Vettam Mani

   o A comprehensive reference work on the Puranas, offering an in-depth look at their characters, themes, and teachings, including those from the *Agni Purana*.

5. **Hindu Rituals and Practices** by Swami Sivananda

   o A detailed guide to Hindu religious practices, this book explains the significance of yajnas, agnihotras, and other rituals associated with Agni.

6. **The Concept of God in Hinduism** by S. Radhakrishnan

   o This philosophical work delves into the nature of divine manifestations in Hinduism, including the elemental and symbolic representations of Agni.

7. **Fire and Sacrifice: The Rites of Agni** by A.K. Ramanujan

   o This book explores the role of fire rituals in Hinduism, particularly in relation to Agni as both a deity and a symbol, drawing connections to the *Agni Purana*.

8. **The Upanishads** (translated by Eknath Easwaran, Swami Prabhavananda, and others)

- The Upanishads offer profound spiritual wisdom that complements the teachings of the *Agni Purana*, especially regarding the nature of fire as a metaphor for the divine and the process of inner transformation.

9. **Hindu Mythology, Vedic and Puranic** by W. J. Wilkins

   - A comprehensive exploration of Hindu mythology, this book provides detailed accounts of deities, stories, and cosmological concepts from the Puranas, including the *Agni Purana*.

10. **The Art of Hindu Ritual** by David Kinsley

    - A scholarly work examining the ritualistic practices in Hinduism, including the significance of fire ceremonies and the symbolic presence of Agni in these rituals.

11. **Agni: The Vedic Fire God** by S. R. Bhatt

    - This book specifically focuses on the worship and symbolism of Agni in Vedic texts and its evolution in later Puranic literature, offering insights relevant to the *Agni Purana*.

12. **Puranic Texts and Rituals** by J. L. Shastri

    - A detailed study of the Puranic texts and their connection to Hindu rituals, with a focus on the role of Agni and fire-based worship.

13. **The Philosophy of the Upanishads** by Paul Deussen

    - A philosophical exploration of the Upanishads that also illuminates the broader spiritual context in which fire rituals, including those described in the *Agni Purana*, are practiced.

14. **The Hindu Way of Life** by Mahatma Gandhi

    - Gandhi's interpretation of Hindu teachings, focusing on simplicity, purity, and devotion—concepts that align closely with the moral principles found in the *Agni Purana*.

15. **The History of Hinduism** by Thomas R. Trautmann

    - This book offers a historical perspective on the development of Hindu thought, including the impact of the Puranas on the religious practices and worldview of the Hindu community.

16. **The Symbolism of Fire in Religion** by Mircea Eliade

    - A cross-cultural study of the symbolism of fire in various religious traditions, offering insights into how fire serves as a transformative and divine force, akin to the role of Agni in Hinduism.

These texts, ranging from ancient scriptures to contemporary analyses, provide a rich foundation for exploring the vast and intricate teachings of the *Agni Purana* and its lasting influence on Hindu philosophy, rituals, and spirituality.

Made in the USA
Las Vegas, NV
21 May 2025

22466484R00044